Cooperative Parenting™ *& Divorce*

"Shielding Your Child From Conflict"

A Parent Guide to Effective Co-Parenting

Susan Blyth Boyan, M.Ed., L.M.F.T.
Ann Marie Termini, M.S., L.P.C

ACTIVE PARENTING™ PUBLISHERS
www.activeparenting.com

ISBN 1-880283-26-3

Dear Parent,

During the process of divorce, you may be struggling to redefine your relationship with your former spouse as well as helping your child cope with the separation of the family. Your struggle is probably magnified by anger, pain and the lack of knowledge regarding how to support yourself and your child during this trying time. By purchasing this book you have taken the first step in facing the challenges associated with divorce. We commend you for your willingness to meet your challenges head-on and applaud your efforts as you take steps to positively influence the process of divorce for both yourself and your child.

This guide offers valuable information about the process of divorce and practical skills necessary to create a two household family. It not only addresses children's issues associated with divorce, but it focuses on you and your personal struggle to overcome the loss of your marriage. In addition, the eight steps to a healthier post-divorce relationship will help you create a partnership in parenting with your former spouse on your child's behalf. You will discover valuable information about divorce, practical suggestions and effective activities to reinforce new skills.

Throughout this guide, you will be asked to make some difficult changes in your relationship with your former spouse in order to reduce problems for your child. Likewise, you will be challenged to take a "leap of faith" and focus on positive ways to interact with your co-parent. We realize how difficult this may be, particularly for those parents who have been divorced a long time. However, recognizing that parental conflict is detrimental to your child's healthy adjustment, will help you make a commitment to remain child-focused, manage your anger, take control of conflict and negotiate child-friendly agreements.

As you journey through this book, you will soon discover that you have the power to make positive changes that will benefit your child and your long-term relationship with your child's other parent. Although it is ideal for both parents to read and complete the activities, you can however make improvements in your current situation even if the other parent chooses not to join you in your efforts.

When you give your child/ren the gift of a strong co-parent relationship and a healthy two home family, you are truly giving them one of the best gifts a parent can ever give. By following the suggestions in this book, you are dedicating yourself to this important goal. By committing to care, you will give your child the gift of love, continued contact with both parents and a happier childhood. Through you, your child can learn that he or she still has a family with two loving parents.

You may be choosing to read this voluntarily or you may be purchasing it as part of your court order requiring you and the former spouse to participate in the Cooperative Parenting and Divorce program.* In either case, you have taken an important first step in facing the challenges associated with divorce.

Wishing you strength, courage and patience as you move forward in establishing a cooperative parenting relationship.

Sincerely,

Susan Boyan and Ann Marie Termini

*This parent guide is used in *Cooperative Parenting and Divorce* groups. It is also sold as a stand-alone text. For more information contact Active Parenting Publishers at 1-800-825-0060.

Table of Contents

1.

Child Focused or Out of Focus

Making The Commitment to Caring

1.

Making the Commitment to Caring
(Child Focused or Out of Focus)

"Honey, I need to talk to you. Your father and I have been having a lot of problems lately and . . . we've decided to get a divorce."

Divorce: Other than birth itself, divorce may be the most significant event in the life of a child who experiences it. It's the knife that slashes not only his family but his world into pieces. It's the event which affects most physical aspects of his life: where he lives, with whom he lives, who he tells about his day. And it has the capacity for affecting most emotional aspects of his life: his confidence level, his self-esteem, his skill for dealing with problems and relationships.

How will the life of this child be affected? Will he successfully recover from the event that shook his foundations and go on to lead a fully productive life? Will she learn to meet life's challenges, overcome life's defeats, develop her talents, build her confidence and self-esteem, develop close, long-lasting personal relationships? Or will she be scarred permanently from the wounds of divorce?

Will he become perpetually sad, withdrawn, depressed? Will she see feedback as criticism and problems as threats to be met with hostility and anger? Will he be afraid to leave relationships that are harmful to him or will he control everyone around him? Will she lack the confidence to pursue her dreams and settle for far less than her birthright allowed? Will he or she find drugs and alcohol key to minimizing the pain inflicted by the divorce?

What Makes The Difference?

Which direction will be his or her destiny? And why does one child heal from the wounds of divorce with little scarring while another becomes permanently disfigured? Research shows that many factors determine a child's reactions to divorce. Some are inherent and cannot be altered, such as the child's age at the time of the divorce, the child's gender and temperament. Other factors, however, can be controlled. And the control for those factors is held in the hands of the child's parents.

You probably aren't aware that you have the capacity to influence your child's long-term recovery from the injury of divorce. You may not know what to do or how you can positively influence his or her future. You are certain of one fact, however, you love your child and would do anything in your power to ensure his or her well-being.

Parents do care; they care tremendously. There is no doubt that parents make decisions, take risks, and meet challenges in the best interest of their children. The decision itself to divorce may have been taken in order to protect him or her from the ongoing battle during the marriage.

Child Focused or Out of Focus?

Although you may differ from other parents who are reading this book in age, background, or even in some of your values, you probably share with them one central belief: You love your child and would not knowingly do anything to hurt him or her. This strongly held belief is so important to your child's success and yours that we want to keep this image clearly in focus as you journey through this book. To keep the focus on the love you have for your child(ren), carry out the following activity.

Child Focus Activity

Find a photo of each of your children and paste it in the frame below. (or use the inside front cover if you have several children). It can be a current school photo that shows the child's missing teeth or perhaps it's a favorite photo of your child when he/she was an infant. It might show you holding or interacting with your child, or your child's face might fill the entire frame. Do this now.

Did you complete this activity? It might not seem like much, but it really is in your child's best interest that you follow through. Return here often. Use this page as a starting place whenever you're in doubt, need encouragement, or need a reminder of the reason for your decision to improve your situation. It will serve as your focal point when you're evaluating decisions, your touchstone when finding your direction, your mission or purpose when you're choosing your day-to-day actions.

Before we go on, there's another activity that complements the last one. In the space provided, think of all the reasons why you would do whatever it takes to protect your child from harm and ensure his or her long-term physical and mental well-being. They can be general reasons ("I want him to grow up with confidence") or specific reasons ("I suffered from a lot of insecurities when my own parents divorced and I don't want her to suffer in the same way"). There are no right or wrong answers here.

"Five Reasons" Activity

List five reasons you would do whatever it takes to protect your child/ren from harm and ensure his/her long-term well-being:

1. _____

2. _____

3. _____

4. _____

5. _____

Remembering...

Pause for a minute to remember what it was like when your child was first born. Picture your infant in those first few months looking up at you with eyes that told you she was perfectly happy snuggled in your protective arms. Remember what your baby looked like when she was sleeping, or smiling at you with that perfect grin.

Think about how much your child depended on you to keep him safe. Remember how you ran toward the road to prevent her from getting hit by a car. Remember how you faithfully strapped her in her car seat, insuring her safety should another driver exercise poor judgment.

Think about the ways your child imitated your behavior, repeating your words and copying your actions whether you were vacuuming the floor or shaving in front of the mirror. Remember how your child ran into your arms when you had been gone at work for all of one day.

When we trace our steps back to the beginning, it's easy to remember the significant role we played in our child's life and how important our every smile, word and deed were to our youngsters. It may not be so easy to distinguish the degree of your influence today, especially if he is older or you aren't the custodial parent. However, be assured that your role, influence and significance remain enormous throughout your child's life.

And because your actions influence him so enormously, they can guide him either toward a healthy recovery from the shock of divorce or toward more serious consequences in her long-term emotional health. That's what this book is all about—to help you understand just how your actions influence his future development and to learn how to use that power to influence it positively. The next section explains in more detail just how this happens.

Why Conflict Hurts

Some children escape the trauma of divorce nearly unscathed, adjusting quickly to their new circumstances and going on to function well throughout adulthood. Others, however, are severely scarred by the experience and exhibit a multitude of problems years after the divorce. What makes the difference?

Research indicates there are a number of factors which influence the child's adjustment to divorce:

Age of the child

As the chart at the end of the chapter shows, the age of the child at the time of the divorce seems to affect the child's reaction to it. In general, children under five show their pain the most keenly at the time of the divorce but adjust best of all the age groups. They have fewer memories of their birth family and make the transition to step-families well.

Children in the next age group, 5–12 years old, generally react with hostility in the immediate aftermath of the divorce. Many signs indicate the degree of stress these children experience, with the most telling, perhaps, being the frequency with which their academic grades plummet the first year after the family breakup.

Teenagers don't wear their feelings on their sleeves, but there is often turmoil hidden underneath. Adolescents navigate the treacherous waters of divorce with trepidation, already dealing with the normal insecurities of peer relationships, sexuality, obsession about their bodies and normal separation from parents. The added stress of divorce at this time can precipitate serious consequences. Some act out, battling everyone and everything around them; others turn the battle inward and become acutely depressed.

So while age does not determine the long-term mental well-being of the child, it does profoundly influence the child's reaction to it.

Gender

The child's gender may indicate differences in his or her response to the divorce. Research shows that, in the first few years following the divorce, boys often have more difficulties in social and personal adjustment as well as in academic performance. However, long-term studies show that girls who appear at the time to adjust well to the divorce have more significant problems later on.

Temperament

A more consistent finding is the adjustment made by children with differing temperaments. The child who has an easygoing personality or temperament from birth, who has always adjusted easily to new food, strange places, and the next developmental stage, also adjusts well to the disruptions caused by the divorce. This "resiliency" characteristic allows them to move between households with minimal difficulty and to flexibly adjust to new patterns. Children on the other end of the scale, the "reactive" children, fare less well. These children (who were often colicky infants) who navigated each developmental stage as though they were in stormy waters are more inflexible when faced with the changes forced upon them by divorce. For these youngsters, divorce is a difficult life experience.

These factors—age, gender and temperament—are all inherent factors; they can't be altered or controlled. However, there are 2 additional factors which can not only be controlled but also have more influence on the child's long-term adjustment than these other factors combined. **These factors are the parent's emotional stability and the amount of conflict in the relationship of the child's parents.**

Parental Functioning

A parent may be in so much personal pain that they unintentionally neglect their child's needs. On the other hand, some parents feel so much guilt and anxiety for their children that they become overindulgent and lose the ability to provide continued structure and support.

If a parent becomes stuck in the grief process (such as anger or depression) their pain may be mirrored by their children. These parents may also seek emotional support from their children which increases a child's anxiety and sense of parental responsibility.

Parents with underlying emotional or addiction problems, such as chronic depression are at risk and may suffer a greater decline in their functioning. Consequently, their children may experience an additional loss; the loss of a healthy parent.

It is crucial that children receive support as they cope with the separation of the family. Children make a better adjustment if at least one parent can provide their child extra support and guidance during this trying time. Parents need to provide continued discipline, support and routine in order to create a stable environment.

Conflict Between Parents

Many couples experience hostility in the first year or two following the break-up. Often it is intense before resolving itself into a low level of tension. However, for some couples, the conflict drags on and on and settles into a pattern that emerges repeatedly. Years later, these couples still cannot be in the same room without problems erupting. Other couples experience an intensity of conflict that does not subside.

Every level of hostility breeds painful consequences for the children. The more intense the conflict, the greater the potential for damage. And the longer it lasts, the greater the chance of a child who is severely marred. When both of these factors—a lengthened period of hostility and high intensity of conflict—are present, the children experience severe disruption, even into their adult lives. It is these divorces which produce children at great risk of long-term injury.

How Conflict Hurts

This discussion of parental conflict may seem very confusing. After all, the conflict occurs between the parents, not between the parent and the child. So how can it hurt the child? To understand how that happens, we have to understand something about the developmental influences on children. The following anecdotes will set the stage for this understanding.

Diminishes the parents' role as "protector"

> Rachel and her father, Robert, have had a fun weekend together. When Robert returns Rachel to the house where Rachel and her mother, Jackie, live, she immediately confronts him about her overdue support check. The confrontation quickly turns into attack and counterattack as Jackie and Robert volley verbal arrows at one another at the top of their voices. When their voices reach a crescendo, Rachel manages to "hurt herself," drawing their attention back to her.

What Jackie and Robert don't realize is the systematic damage they are doing to one of the most important parental functions: that of "protector." When children are young, the intensity of their own feelings can frighten them. They run screaming to Mommy or Daddy when they skin a knee or are faced with monsters in the dark. Mommy or Daddy calm their fears and soothe their anxieties, thus providing a kind of protection against real or imagined dangers.

Even into adulthood well-adjusted individuals look to close family members when they're upset, welcoming a parent's reminder that "Everything will be all right." However, in divorces where the parents long exhibit intense hostility toward one another, the parents themselves are the ones upset and out of control. They exhibit their own fears, anxieties and intense anger on repeated occasions.

This is terribly unsettling to the child. If the parent acts like a child in managing his or her emotions and appears to require protection him/herself, who will protect the child from all those dangers? Who will soothe and comfort him and help him learn to handle his own anxieties? Who will provide the security net against real and imagined monsters if the parent is in need of protection too? When the parent can't perform that function, the child is laid open to extreme levels of anxiety and doubt. He can no longer count on the security of a firm foundation found in his birth family. It's hard for him to build his own confidence on a foundation of quicksand.

Complicates the child's role identity

> Eleven-year-old Tanya arrives at her Dad's house. James, her father, greets her: "Hey, you're right on time. Great. We can get to the gym before it gets too busy. Did you remember your bathing suit this time? Oh no, not again. You forgot again? We had planned to go tonight. Why can't you remember a simple thing like that?" Disappointedly, he adds, "You're just like your mother."

What started out as a positive, shared time between James and Tanya has suddenly changed into a disappointment for James and an emotional quagmire for Tanya. By reminding Tanya that she's like her mother in ways that he hates, James is not only criticizing Tanya but threatening her self-esteem. After all, he divorced Tanya's mother because he doesn't love her anymore. Tanya could interpret that message as "I'm like Mother, who's not worthy of love; therefore I'm not worthy of love." After all, the child is a product of the union of both her parents; therefore, she is already like her mother in many ways. She's female, shares the characteristic of being forgetful, and may share other physical features or personality traits as well.

When James compares Tanya to her mother at a time when he's disapproving of her mother, he is in effect telling Tanya that she is "not good enough." What will happen when Tanya approaches the next challenge and thinks to herself, "I'm not good enough"? She is likely to make a half-hearted attempt to meet the challenge, thereby dooming herself to failure and thus proving to herself that she's not, in fact, good enough.

A second problem for Tanya is her "role identity" with her mother. Tanya's mother is her first role model for how a female is supposed to act. If Tanya hears many messages of disapproval regarding her mother, she can become confused about how she is supposed to act in her female capacity. Should she act like her mother, her closest female role model, or should she not act like her mother in ways that demonstrate her gender? If she does, she may be disapproved of herself, but if she doesn't, she is rejecting the female role model that is closest to her.

Fails to teach effective conflict-resolution skills (Promotes poor conflict-resolution skills)

Sarah is fourteen. Her parents are discussing her upcoming vacation plans. Her father wants to leave on Thursday to catch an early flight to Florida. Sarah's mother fights the idea since officially the father's time with her doesn't start until 3:00 on Friday. The disagreement quickly escalates to a shouting match, with each side thrusting and jabbing at any weaknesses in the other's character traits as well. When she can't stand anymore of it, Sarah retreats to her room.

There's an old saying that goes, "Parents are a child's first teacher." If that is so, what are these parents teaching their teen? First, how to turn a small difference of opinion into a major problem. Second, to back every problem with an argument. Third, how to turn a problem into character assassination. And fourth, how to win at any cost.

If the teen learns well from her role models, she too can turn her own problems with people into opportunities for creating conflict. She too can prevent problems from finding solutions, and negotiations from forming agreements.

All she has to do is be a good student.

Threatens loss of stability or abandonment

Six-year-old Rachel excitedly waits for her Daddy to arrive. They're going to the zoo, Rachel's favorite Saturday activity. When Robert arrives five minutes early, Rachel's mother, Jackie, refuses to open the door because, officially, Robert's visitation doesn't start yet. That tease pushes Robert's button and he goes into a fury. First he threatens, then goes into a rage when the appointed time finally comes, his anger results in knocking over a plant. Verbal threats reach an ever-increasing level on both sides until Robert nearly strikes Jackie, stopped only by the thought of his daughter listening in the other room. Robert hastily retreats and disappears out the door with his daughter's words, "Daddy, Daddy, I want my Daddy," ringing in his ears.

While the threat of violence is a real danger to the normal development of a child's personality, the fear of abandonment can be just as terrifying. Being left alone to fend for oneself is a deeply disturbing thought. Since they can't provide for themselves, children know instinctively that they're dependent on the adults around them. Their survival depends on it. Therefore anything that threatens the stability of keeping the close adults in their lives threatens their emotional welfare at the most basic level.

Adults often use the phrase, "He/she's always there for me," when they're describing a close relationship. Even though they have the capacity to care for themselves, adults too are uneasy about facing problems by themselves. So it's not surprising that the threat of being abandoned strikes terror in the heart of a child.

There's another dilemma here too. Rachel is frightened of being abandoned by her father but she's also angry at her mother for her role in the conflict. However, she doesn't dare show her anger because she too could leave. That puts her in the middle of a very frustrating situation. If she expresses her anger at her mother, it could hurt her more. If she doesn't get to express these negative feelings, the pressure could build until there's an explosion.

Puts the child in a loyalty bind

Marcus has just opened his birthday gift from his father, Charles. It's a skateboard.

Although it's the one thing he passionately wanted for his birthday, no smile lights up his face. When his father, disappointed with his son's lack of enthusiasm, inquires, Marcus reveals the reason for his sad face: His mother's firm refusal to allow her son to have a skateboard. She thinks they're unsafe and she has voiced this opinion to both Marcus and Charles.

Charles is furious at his former wife's interference, loudly proclaiming that his son will not only keep the skateboard but will proudly take it home with him and use it whenever he wants. The expression on Marcus's face is filled with anguish.

Whether they realize it or not, parents have great influence on their children. Their values, beliefs, and standards all help a child set his own limits and influence his opinions. Children may argue but they are usually loyal followers of parental rules and underlying values. What happens, then, when divorced parents disagree vehemently and put their children in the middle of the fight? The child is placed in a huge **loyalty bind**. This forces the child to choose between one parent or the other. He's caught in the middle with no way out. Whichever way he turns he's forced to make a decision which will turn one parent against him. He believes that he can't be loyal to both. The situation forces him to take an action which will only end up causing pain.

What could be the long-term consequences? What happens if he gets used to choosing the side that causes him pain? He might choose the side of crime, of addiction, of promiscuity. After all it's the pattern he was taught by his parents.

You've Got The Power

If you're concerned about the long-term consequences of conflict on your own child, what can you do about it? Through your special relationship to your child, you have the power to influence your child's well-being either positively or negatively. As a matter of fact, the only two individuals who have this power are the same two individuals who have the power to improve the way problems are handled today. Either singly or together you can make a commitment to alter the amount of conflict in your child's life. No one can do it for you. No one can make you. You have to individually decide if you want to alter the pattern of tension and hostility that surrounds your child and interferes with his or her happiness.

You might be thinking that if only the other parent would change, things could be better right away. There's a problem with that way of thinking: it leads us right back to where we are. It's like the old saying, "Insanity is when you keep doing what you've been doing but you expect a different result." The only way you'll get something better for your child is if you do something different.

Take The Lead

In a way, relationships can be like dancing. If you lead, the other person has to follow. But it won't be easy. If you've ever changed your steps in the middle of the dance, what happened? Confusion and resistance at first. Your partner tried to get you to go back to the way you were doing things. However, if you persist, he or she picks up the new method and gets in step with you once again.

What Is the Sound of One Hand Clapping?

It's a cliché but it's still true: When it comes to arguing, it takes two. One can't do it alone. If you're the one who takes your "sails" out of the other person's "wind," all the huffing and puffing done by your child's other parent won't blow you off course. Think about it: you control the interaction when you decide whether or not you're going to participate. The question still remains: Are you ready to commit to taking the lead, to acting alone if necessary, to reduce the conflict if it's good for your child?

What Stops You? What's The Cost?

You may still feel a twinge realizing something is holding you back. You have a suspicion that you may have to give up something in order to get something. Conflict has a high cost to both the parents and the child. It costs the child security, self-esteem, confidence, emotional control, happiness, normal personality development and a range of other considerations. However, it may surprise you to learn that the conflict is also costly to the parents in terms of level of happiness, anxiety, discomfort and a host of disturbances which limit a full and productive life.

What's The Benefit?

You may also realize that parents benefit more from the conflict than the child. That, of course, is why parents keep it going. Which of the following benefits might be true for you?

- The sense of power?
- The fun of competition?
- The satisfaction of revenge?
- The pleasure of fighting to win?
- The satisfaction of being right?
- The satisfaction or pleasure of blaming the co-parent for the sad state of affairs?
- The convenience of not taking responsibility for your life?

- The reward of playing the a victim?
- The desire to stay connected to the co-parent even if only through conflict?
- The challenge, or even a purpose in life?
- To avoid fear of change?

What's The Cost For Cooperating?

Both parents and children benefit from a cooperative parental relationship. Both receive the advantages of lower stress, reduced anger, less tension and a more peaceful existence. While both parents and children receive benefits, it is the parents who bear the cost. What is the cost for cooperating? Parents have to give up the blame game and start taking responsibility for their own happiness. That's a tough stand and, for some, it's easier just to keep the fight going. But notice who pays the price: **the child**.

Is It Worth It?

Is it worth giving up anger and blame in order to ensure your child an improved chance for happiness and success in life?

Leap Of Faith

Making the commitment to a new parental relationship means leaving something behind in order to get something better for yourself and your child. But it comes with a risk. You have to get out of the old pattern and try something different. You have to leave your comfort zone and forge into the unknown. It requires a leap of faith. Have you ever seen a squirrel run up a tree and scamper out to the end of the branch, readying itself to jump to the branch on the next tree? To get what he wants, the squirrel has to leave the safety of his old position; he has to take that leap of faith. When parents want to get something better for their children, they too must take that leap.

Making The Commitment To Caring

There is no doubt that you love your child. You have always done your best to make the best decisions for your child. This is your opportunity to make another decision that is good for your child. Choose to "Make a Commitment to Caring." Choose to do whatever it takes to improve the long-term well-being of your child. Look back at the picture of your child at the beginning of this chapter. Is he or she worth it? You decide. If you are willing to make a commitment to your child you will be placing him or her on the first step to long-term well-being.

The remaining chapters in this book will guide you in taking the seven additional steps to achieve this goal. On page 13 you will see an outline of these steps.

**STOP READING AND COMPLETE THE
"COMMITMENT TO CARING" ON THE NEXT PAGE.**

Commit to Care

I _____, parent of _____
     (Your Name)   *(Child/ren's Name)*

make a commitment to the long term mental health of my child/ren. I
agree to take the lead to do whatever is necessary to reduce conflict
and tension between myself and _____. I
                                     (Co-Parent's Name)
am sincerely committed to loving my child/ren. I realize that to be a
good parent I must give up my negative and destructive behaviors. I
realize these behaviors will only damage my child's well being.

Even if _____ does not make this
                (Co-Parent's Name)
commitment, I can still be effective in making a difference in the
patterns of our relationship. However, this will not mean that I will
give in to unusual demands nor does it mean that I will fight to win.
It does mean that I will avoid any conflict in my child's presence and
follow the divorce rules at all times. I will learn and practice new
techniques for handling situations that create problems. Changing
will not be easy. However, I will do this for _____.
                                       (Child/ren's Name)
Because I love my child, I will take this action willingly.

Parent Signature _____

Date _____

8 STEPS
TO MY CHILD'S
POSITIVE MENTAL HEALTH
AND WELL-BEING

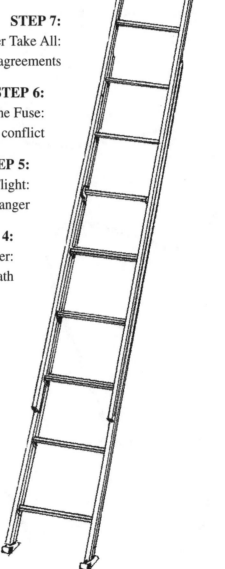

STEP 8:
Cooperation or Conflict:
Co-parenting is forever

STEP 7:
All a Winner or Winner Take All:
Negotiating agreements

STEP 6:
Defuse or Light the Fuse:
Taking control of conflict

STEP 5:
Neither Fight nor Take Flight:
Managing my own anger

STEP 4:
Make It Better or Keep It Bitter:
Choosing my personal path

STEP 3:
Letting Go or Holding On:
Changing my long-term role

STEP 2:
Plan for Peace or Tug of War:
Allowing my child to love both parents

STEP 1:
Child Focused or Out of Focus:
Making the commitment to caring

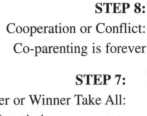

 # Exercises

Hopes and Dreams

Directions: On this page is an illustration that represents your children. Take a few minutes to write down all the hopes and dreams you have for your child inside the figure. For instance, you may hope that your child has a positive self-esteem and continued good health. Perhaps your dream for your child is a great education and fulfilling career. Some examples might include tolerance of frustration, perseverance, confidence, impulse control, discipline, responsibility and spirituality.

Create an Action Plan

Directions: Look back at the your "Hopes and Dreams" on the previous page. Put your commitment to caring into action by creating an action plan for making your dreams become a reality. First, determine how your behaviors are **interfering** with any of your goals for your child. For example, your child will not develop impulse control if you cannot model control when you are interacting with the other parent. As you progress through the next seven chapters you will learn alternative behaviors and the skills to put your action plan into gear. For now, just list the goals in the left column that you may be interfering with. Then add any **of your behaviors** that may interfere with your child's positive development and the goals. As you learn new skills, replace your current inappropriate behaviors with alternative behaviors that will positively influence your child's development. The first one has been done for you.

GOAL/DREAM	MY DAMAGING BEHAVIOR	ALTERNATIVE POSITIVE
1. My child will have a positive self-esteem.	I make negative comments about the other parent when my child can overhear these comments. This will damage my child's self-esteem.	I will stop making negative comments in front of my child. When I need to share my feelings, I will call a friend.
2.		
3.		
4.		
5.		
6.		
7.		

Love Isn't Easy.....How Far Will You Go?

Directions: Slowly read each question asking yourself, "How far will I go?" Answer honestly. You will notice that the first five questions present easier decisions because they indicate eminent physical danger while the last five present emotional danger. Are you willing to risk placing your child in danger of any kind?

1. Would you jump into an ice-cold stream to save your child from drowning?

2. Would you give up one of your kidneys if it would save your child's life?

3. Would you sell all your worldly possessions for costly life-saving surgery for your child?

4. Would you change your diet if your child's doctor diagnosed your child with diabetes?

5. Would you give up smoking if your child had a high risk of lung disease or asthma?

6. Would you forgive your child's other parent to help your child develop a healthy self-esteem?

7. Would you let go of the past to give your child a positive future?

8. Would you let go of bitterness/anger if your child developed anxiety symptoms?

9. Would you use impulse control if it would teach your child to think before he acted?

10. Would you give up being right so your child wouldn't feel caught in the middle?

**Love is action . . . not words!
If you really love your child,
it is time to ACT like it.**

Make your child's dreams a reality.

Divorce Rules

Directions: Post these rules on your refrigerator as a reminder of your commitment to care. Ask your child to let you know if you forget one of the rules. Never reprimand your child when he or she gives you this feedback.

Dear Mom and Dad, I'm just a kid, so please . . .

1. Do not talk badly about my other parent. *(This makes me feel torn apart! It also makes me feel bad about myself!)*

2. Do not talk about my other parent's friends or relatives. *(Let me care for someone even if you don't.)*

3. Do not talk about the divorce or other grown-up stuff. *(This makes me feel sick. Please leave me out of it!)*

4. Do not talk about money or child support. *(This makes me feel guilty or like I'm a possession instead of your kid.)*

5. Do not make me feel bad when I enjoy my time with my other parent. *(This makes me afraid to tell you things.)*

6. Do not block my visits or prevent me from speaking to my other parent on the phone. *(This makes me very upset.)*

7. Do not interrupt my time with my other parent by calling too much or by planning my activities during our time together.

8. Do not argue in front of me or on the phone when I can hear you! *(This just turns my stomach inside out!)*

9. Do not ask me to spy for you when I am at my other parent's home. *(This makes me feel disloyal and dishonest.)*

10. Do not ask me to keep secrets from my other parent. *(Secrets make me feel anxious.)*

11. Do not ask me questions about my other parent's life or about our time together. *(This makes me uncomfortable. So just let me tell you.)*

12. Do not give me verbal messages to deliver to my other parent. *(I end up feeling anxious about their reaction. So please just call them, leave them a message at work or put a note in the mail.)*

13. Do not send written messages with me or place them in my bag. *(This also makes me uncomfortable.)*

14. Do not blame my other parent for the divorce or for things that go wrong in your life. *(This really feels terrible! I end up wanting to defend them from your attack. Sometimes it makes me feel sorry for you and that makes me want to protect you. I just want to be a kid, so please, please . . . stop putting me into the middle!)*

15. Do not treat me like an adult, it causes way too much stress for me. *(Please find a friend or therapist to talk with.)*

16. Do not ignore my other parent or sit on opposite sides of the room during my school or sports activities. *(This makes me very sad and embarrassed. Please act like parents and be friendly, even if it is just for me.)*

17. Do let me take items to my other home as long as I can carry them back and forth. *(Otherwise it feels like you are treating me like a possession.)*

18. Do not use guilt to pressure me to love you more and do not ask me where I want to live.

19. Do realize that I have two homes, not just one. *(It doesn't matter how much time I spend there.)*

20. Do let me love both of you and see each of you as much as possible! Be flexible even when it is not part of our regular schedule.

Thanks, your loving child

My Parenting Concerns

List any parenting concerns that you have for your child. Be sure to list only issues that affect your child directly. For instance, parenting concerns may include: 1) my child's other parent does not call our child when he says he will, or 2) my child's other parent attempts to argue with me in front of our children. Continue to use this page to record your parenting concerns while you are reading this book. Issues that affect you personally should be listed on page 201 near the end of this book, "TRASH IT HERE."

My Parenting Concerns *(continuation)*

A Child's Reactions To Divorce

Infants & Toddlers:

Reactions:

- loss of developmental accomplishments (return to bottle/crawling, waking in the night)
- highly reactive to their environment
- may become angry when their needs are overlooked or when caretaking schedules are unpredictable
- demonstrates fear by clinging to parent and refusing to separate from parent
- exhibits intense feelings of frustration and anger through biting, hitting, throwing toys
- may not interact with adult caregivers
- loss of interest in exploring their environment

What to do:

- make sure the daily routine is reasonably consistent
- initially keep child-care arrangements intact
- maintain consistent drop-off and pick-up times from day care
- allow your child to take two or three familiar objects to the day-care setting
- keep in mind that long separations from the primary parent may be highly distressing for the child
- reduce parental hostilities

Preschool:

Reactions:

- loss of developmental accomplishments (return to bottle, soiling self, baby talk, etc.)
- confusion over the cause of the divorce and how it will affect their own life
- belief that they are responsible for the divorce
- fears of rejection and abandonment
- separation anxiety
- may exhibit anger and aggression toward other children or siblings
- temper tantrums may increase
- more possessive of personal items
- may cry frequently
- difficulty sleeping
- loss of interest in pleasurable activities
- may appear joyless, listless and withdrawn

What to do:

- frequently reassure your children that they will be taken care of and that their parents still love them
- provide an opportunity for your child to share his fears and concerns
- allow your child to spend meaningful one-on-one time with each parent as often as possible
- initially keep child-care arrangements intact
- provide a reassuring sense of consistency (daily activities, bedtime routine, discipline, etc.)
- minimize the number of negative and positive changes
- reduce parental hostilities

Elementary School Age (six to eight):

Reactions:

- preoccupation with feelings of sadness, loss, rejection and guilt
- may cry easily, act cranky, and be anxious
- distractible; difficulty concentrating
- decline in school performance
- complaints of headaches, stomachaches or other physical complaints
- attempts to actively reunite their parents (sometimes by having problems that force parental involvement)
- may assume the role of the absent parent in order to comfort or support the primary parent
- strong sense of responsibility to take care of their parents

What to do:

- allow your child to love both parents without pressuring them to side with one parent against the other
- avoid criticizing the other parent in front of the child
- reassure your child that you still love them and will take care of them
- let them know that they will still be able to see and visit the parent not living in the family home
- provide a sense of consistency (daily activities, bedtime routines, discipline, etc.)
- minimize the number of positive and negative changes
- reduce parental hostilities

Preteens (nine to twelve):

Reactions:

- may exhibit sadness, loneliness, insecurity, and feelings of helplessness
- attempt to undo the divorce
- tend to feel alone and frightened, but since they are easily embarrassed they may pretend to act cool
- complaints of headaches, stomachaches or other physical complaints
- may take sides and choose one parent over the other
- may feel and express intense anger
- have a strong sense of loyalty and may tend to rescue and side with the "wronged" parent
- may adopt an adult role
- decline in school performance
- friendships may suffer
- may engage in stealing, lying, or refusing to go to school
- may prematurely date and become involved in sexual behavior

What to do:

- talk about the divorce and the changes that will occur, but avoid the legal details
- allow your child to express his fears, concerns, and complaints to each parent
- acknowledge your child's anger and attempt to change those things that the child finds most upsetting
- allow your child to love both parents
- do not pressure your child to choose sides
- reduce parental hostilities

Adolescents:

Reactions:

- less talkative and temporarily withdraw to cope with their feelings and emotions
- exhibit angry and rebellious behavior
- may become sexually active
- may use drugs and alcohol as a way to escape
- decline in school performance
- may become preoccupied with a sense of family
- may adopt an adult role

What to do:

- encourage open and honest communication, but avoid legal details
- encourage your child to ask questions and state their concerns about the departed parent
- avoid relying on your child as a source of emotional support
- reduce parental hostilities

Always:

- encourage open and honest communication between parent and child. Allow your child to express their fears, concerns, and complaints
- answer your child's questions honestly and patiently without providing adult information that would cause undue stress for your child. When your child asks you a question that is difficult to answer due to its personal nature, respond by saying, "It's okay for you to ask me questions. Sometimes I may not give you an answer because I don't feel comfortable sharing it with you at the time. Please respect my privacy and I will respect yours."
- reassure your child that they will be taken care of, that you still love her, and that the divorce was not her fault
- minimize positive and negative change. As much as possible maintain the same residence, school, church, and child-care facilities
- help your child maintain contact with extended family and friends
- prepare your child for changes before they happen
- permit your child to love both parents
- provide a stable and secure home by practicing consistent discipline, maintaining rules and limits and consistent daily routines and schedules
- a child at any age may become overly compliant, cooperative and ideal. This should not be seen as a positive reaction

Sources

- Arbuthnot, J. & Gordon, D.A. (1993). Children in the middle. Athens, Ohio: Center for Divorce Education

- Berger, S. (1983). Divorce Without Victims. Boston: Houghton Mifflin Company.

- Clapp, G. (1992). Divorce & New Beginnings. New York: John Wiley & Sons, Inc.

- Kalter, N. (1990). Growing Up With Divorce. New York: The Free Press.

- Marston, S. (1994). The Divorced Parent. New York: William Morrow & Company, Inc.

YOUR CHILD'S SELF ESTEEM!

Dear Mom and Dad,

Thanks for taking the time to help me. This divorce stuff is really hard! Sometimes it makes my tummy hurt! I can't always tell you how I feel. Sometimes I act out my feelings without words. When you talk badly about each other, I feel just awful! Sometimes you both get so angry that you forget I am around. I'm really glad that you are going to help me feel better. Thanks!

Your loving but sad child,

XXXXXOOOOOXXXXX

Chapter One Review

1. Why is it important to keep child-focused when you are dealing with your child's other parent?

2. How is your child affected by parental conflict?

3. In what way might you be benefitting from staying in conflict with your child's other parent?

4. What is a "loyalty bind?"

5. Are any of your behaviors interfering with your "Hopes and Dreams" for your child? If so, what are they?

6. Are you committed to the "Divorce Rules?"

7. Are you open to feedback from your child/ren if you forget one of the "Divorce Rules?"

2.

Plan For Peace or Tug of War

Allowing My Child to Love Both Parents

2.

Allowing My Child to Love Both Parents
(Plan for Peace or Tug of War)

Forced to Choose

Imagine you're 23 years old and you and your boyfriend or girlfriend have decided to get married. You call your parents to share the good news and excitedly await their heartfelt congratulations. Instead of matching your enthusiasm with their own, they act disappointed in your decision. They question your choice of mate and some of their comments could be considered derogatory. As a result, you begin to question your own judgment. You maintain your resolve, however, and continue your plan to wed. As the days progress toward the wedding date, your fiancée and parents start criticizing one another frequently and openly. You feel caught in the middle.

What you looked forward to as the most wonderful time of your life has turned into a tug of war. You are questioning your decision. You feel cheated that your own happiness has been muted. No matter which way you turn you feel resentful that you've been put in this position.

When the situation isn't easily resolved, your stress increases. You want to love both your fiancée and your parents but find it harder and harder to do so. Eventually you feel the need to choose between a continued relationship with your fiancée and with your parents. If you choose your fiancée, you know that your anger toward your parents will rise for putting you in this position. However, you can foresee a time when you would also regret losing your parents, the only two people in your life who can share your earliest life experiences. Then even the presence of your chosen mate will only remind you of the wrenching loss of the two people who loved you and gave you life. It's a no-win situation. You are in a painful **loyalty bind**.

Similarities to Children of Divorce

The situation described above is similar to that of a child with divorced parents who place the child in situations where he gets caught in the middle. At those times the child feels like he is in a tug of war between two battling parents and sometimes has to choose sides. When the child is forced to choose sides, she is prevented from loving both parents. On paper both parents may have equal custody, but in reality, the child feels forced to reject one of them.

Hopefully you have been increasing your awareness about how you put your child into the middle. This chapter will focus on the many ways children feel the stress of being caught in the middle. For example:

One of the most common and frequent occurrences is when **one parent criticizes the other**. Put-downs, criticisms, name-calling and even sighs and eye rolling force the child to side with one parent against the other. It's virtually impossible for the child to stay neutral for reasons we'll discuss later. For now, just remember: **Whenever you attack the other parent, you hurt your own child.**

Another situation where the child is caught in the middle is when the child is asked to deliver a note, a message or the child-support check to the other parent. Once again, the child is put in the middle. If the message or note is likely to upset the parent receiving it, the child will usually be pulled into the fallout which results.

A third common situation which **forces the child to choose one parent over the other** is when the child has a activity that both he and his parents attend, such as a sporting event or school program. Should the child invite both parents, or will the stress of having both warring parties present be so great that the child feels forced to choose only one? The position of having to choose automatically puts the child in the middle.

Children also feel pushed to choose sides when one parent **plays the victim or "poor me" role**. This parent uses guilt to get the child to take her side of the disagreement. The child is put in the middle—between a parent who's a "winner" and one who's a "loser." The parent who talks about how sad he is, how lonely he feels when the child isn't there and how "I've lost everything" puts an incredibly heavy burden on the child. The child is being forced to side with the "victim" against the "winning" parent. The child not only feels hurt but tries to make the parent feel better. The "loser" parent is manipulating the child into fulfilling his own emotional needs. It isn't until later, when the child realizes that the "victim" manipulated her through guilt, that the child becomes resentful for being used in this manner. Although the child wants to freely love both parents, one parent uses the child's vulnerability to pull him in that parent's direction.

Another situation where the child is prevented from loving both parents is when **the parents concentrate too much on making things "equal."** When the child is forced to keep track of hugs, kisses, time, attention and material goods in order to equalize their distribution between the parents, he can't freely demonstrate the love he naturally feels. Every action has to be judged and measured and doled out in equal shares. He can't love both parents with his own free will.

What Happens When a Child is Caught in the Middle?

- First, the child experiences an **increase in stress**. He has to stop his own spontaneous actions due to the need to carefully weigh the consequences. After all, the wrong decision may lead to one of the parents being angry with him. That thought, conscious or unconscious, is terrifying because the child is already experiencing the loss of the parent who has moved out. She also feels betrayed because someone she cares for is forcing her into a position where there's no way out. She's resentful but she can't express anger to the parent. He feels trapped knowing that someone else is controlling his life.

- The second is a general **decrease in the level of happiness**. Caught like a rabbit in a trap, the child isn't free to experience the happiness that other children take for granted. Fearful that a turn in the wrong direction will lead to a parent being hurt, the child tries to avoid choosing sides. Eventually, the child's own stress is too heavy to bear and the child must make a decision and choose one parent or the other. (Do I hand the note to my mother as Dad asked, or do I keep it and face Dad's anger?) One parent is pushed away at least temporarily. The child doesn't have a choice, yet bears the brunt of the result.

- A third result is **a loss of self-esteem**. You see, children aren't fully separated from their parents. They sense that they're somehow connected to their parents as if they are one and the same. The following two large rings on either side represent the child's parents. As you can see by the space between the adults, they are no longer together. The diagram demonstrates the parts that overlap, which gives the child a feeling of connection.

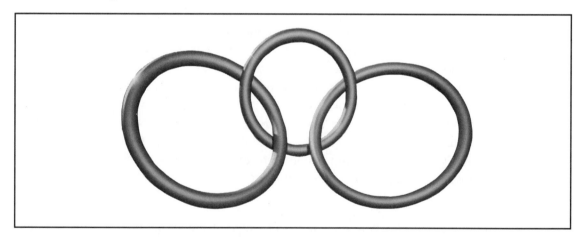

Therefore, if something damages the parent, the child feels damaged too. That's why you'll hear a young child automatically defend his or her parent if the parent has been criticized in some manner. The child feels like he's the one being criticized and he has to defend himself! Criticisms, put-downs and name-calling directed at the other parent are experienced by the child as a direct hit. Of course, the hit isn't physical; it's psychological, and results in the child's loss of self-esteem. See the following diagram.

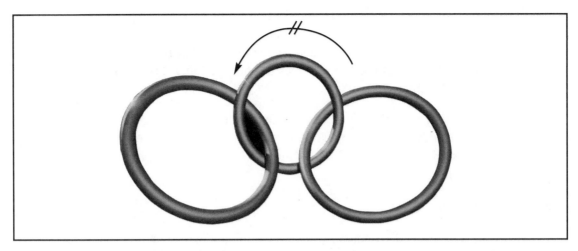

You can imagine the result if the parent is not only "damaged" with criticism but is totally absent. The child feels like a piece of himself is missing too.

He grieves over the loss—not only the loss of the person but the loss of himself. He's never quite complete because there's a gaping hole where a part of him is missing.

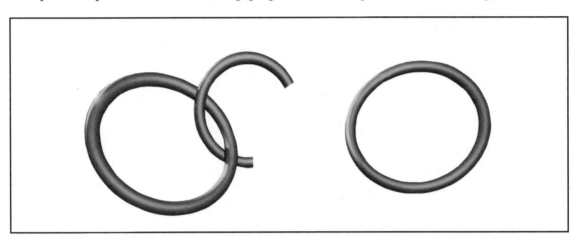

What if There Were Only One Parent?

From the situations described above, you can see how painful the experience is for a child caught in the middle. You might even think about how much easier it would be if you were the only parent involved in the child's life. Think of the advantages: You could eliminate some of your own stress and reduce the need to work out all these details with the child's other parent. You'd have less conflict in your life and all the decisions about the child would be under your direct control.

Even though that scenario might meet your own personal needs, what would be the consequences for your child? Like the 23-year-old in the scenario at the beginning of this chapter who gives up his parents when he sides with his fiancée, the child would miss out on a lot. First, she would miss out on the love of one of the two people closest to her in her life. Secondly he would miss out on the shared memories of his early life which can be provided by only two individuals in the entire world. Third, he would lose out on the sense of value he receives from his important role in the generational process handed down from parent to child.

She'd miss out on the opportunity to discuss her own childhood with both parents and to share those comparisons with both parents when she has a child of her own. He'd miss out on the experience of growing his own independence from the family ties on his own schedule. She'd miss the continuity that her life provides in understanding the characteristics or qualities she shared with the absent parent.

In the same way that the loss of a parent in a child's life is devastating, criticisms of a parent by the child's other parent are also devastating because they force the child to side with one parent, thus rejecting the other. The child is forced to push a parent away and bring the loss upon himself.

Two Are Better Than One

If losing a parent is detrimental, what are the advantages to having two parents involved in a child's life? Since children look to their parents as their first teachers and role models, then it makes sense that two teachers and two role models are better than one. When a child has one role model, the child might get a skewed view of the world, comparing everything else in the world to that one model as the only right way to do things. Having two models gives the child the idea that people in fact differ and there is no single "right" way.

Each parent has qualities, characteristics and interests that are unique to the individual. Having contact with both parents, the child can see a greater variety of qualities, personal characteristics and personal interests. He will be less likely to compare himself to the only adult present in his life. She will be more likely to find herself similar in some ways to one parent and in other ways to the other parent.

In addition, each of the parents offers something special to the child. One parent might be particularly patient, a good listener. Another might be good at providing information on a number of subjects. One might be skillful at car maintenance, another good at math. One might be an excellent role model for caring and support, another could be a good leader and role model for assertiveness skills. One might be a good teacher for cooking or gardening skills, another might be great at sports, or playing a musical instrument. Since each parent brings his or her own special gifts to the parent-child relationship, having two parents doubles the chance that there are good matches between the child's interests and skills and the parents'. If you think about your child's other parent objectively, you can probably think of many characteristics that he or she could contribute in a positive way to parenting. Write those qualities in the following activity. Do that now.

Positive Parenting Qualities

Think of the qualities and characteristics your child's other parent has that can be valued as positive parenting qualities. Write down at least five of these qualities.

1. _____

2. _____

3. _____

4. _____

5. _____

Through Your Child's Eyes

Now take a moment and look at your child's other parent through your child's eyes. What characteristics, qualities and skills do you see that your child might enjoy or admire? Does your child's other parent like to laugh and play silly games? Is she good at math and can help with homework, and later in life provide the child with sound financial advice? Is he creative, musical or a talented Leggo builder? Is she spontaneous, affectionate or organized? Does he enjoy board or computer games? What things would a child enjoy about this person either now or even sometime in the future when the child is in a different stage in life?

Remember you may think making cookies in the kitchen makes a huge mess but your child may think the mess is the best part. If you're an organized planner and your child is a free spirit, your child's other parent might provide a more relaxed environment for your child, while you might be better at helping the child get his homework done on time.

Consider your child's view of his other parent at different stages of his life. Some parents' skills are most valued when a child is young, while others are more appreciated when the child is older. For example, a nurturing adult will be in his element with babies and toddlers while a good conversationalist will likely be more involved with her children later in life. With two adults, there is a greater likelihood that a child will click with at least one parent throughout his different life stages.

Now consider your child's other parent's qualities and characteristics from your **child's point of view**. On the following activity, write down several characteristics or qualities that your child can value or admire, either now or in the future. Be honest. Giving your child's other parent a compliment won't hurt you.

The Other Parent
(As Seen Through My Child's Eyes)

See your child's other parent through the eyes of your child. What qualities, characteristics or skills does he/she have that the child values or admires? Does the parent like to have fun? Is he well organized? Could he share his gardening skills, her tennis skills, his car maintenance interests, her knowledge and enthusiasm for the environment or wildlife? Is he a good listener or is she a dynamic speaker? Write down at least five of the qualities, characteristics or skills that you identified.

1. _____

2. _____

3. _____

4. _____

5. _____

What Can a Parent Do?
Choose When to Show Your Emotions

Now that you're aware that criticisms of your child's other parent hurt your child, you're probably motivated to control your own tendencies to strike out at the other parent. Practice stopping before you lash out at your child's other parent when a maddening situation arises. Think to yourself, **"If I criticize my child's other parent, I'll hurt my own child."** Now pause while you slowly exhale and consider what actions you will take instead.

Remember, stopping and taking a breath doesn't mean that you never have negative emotions. It does mean that you will take a brief moment to consider the consequences of your actions before you take them. It does mean controlling the impulse to strike first and ask questions later. It does mean channeling negative thoughts and feelings into constructive paths that hurt neither you nor your child.

How can you release your anger appropriately without damaging your child? You may need to rely on trusted friends and family members who are willing to listen and let you blow off steam. Talking to them when your child is not within earshot is key. You may choose to find a support group for divorced parents who will more fully appreciate your anger and your self-control. You may want to get into counseling, which can provide a safe place for your anger while you work through difficult moments. All of these are active choices you can make which help prevent open criticism of your child's other parent and the resulting damage to your child.

Stopping and taking a breath to help you catch yourself <u>before acting</u> sounds easy. It isn't. Using this technique may be one of the most difficult tasks you encounter. But it's worth the effort when it keeps your child in a safe position—out of the middle.

Allow Your Child to Love Both Parents

What are some of the actions which allow your child to regain his sense of joy? First, show **acceptance of your child's two homes.** Talk about how he or she now has a family in two locations. Rather than transport everything with the child during visits, keep some clothes and a separate toothbrush at each home. This gesture shows that the child is a permanent resident in each location, not just a visitor or guest. If the child is young, have some toys and creativity supplies at each location, too. If the child is a teenager, she will most likely decide for herself what is best to leave at each home. Encourage keeping some items like music tapes and magazines at each location for the same reason. If you can afford it, having a CD player or tape deck at each house will help a teen feel at home.

Make sure you **create an area for your child in each home.** He needs his own space no matter how limited the room. A dresser, a corner will do. Let the child decide how to decorate that space if possible. Let him know it's all right to bring a picture of his other parent to keep nearby his bed.

Use **language showing acceptance of the other parent.** Your child might overhear you say to a friend something like "Ben is a real math whiz; he got that from Jeremy, his dad." Or you can direct a comment to your daughter like "You've really got your mother's flair for finding good bargains." You'll see the pleasure in your child's eyes not only from the praise but also from the acknowledgment of hearing something positive about his or her other parent.

You'll find that giving your child's other parent a compliment can't hurt you. Instead you'll be proud of what you've done for your child's self-esteem. And that meets your goal.

Earlier you listed some of the other parent's characteristics or qualities that can be seen as positive, either through your eyes or your child's eyes. Review that list now. Find an opportunity to weave a comment about one of these characteristics into your conversation with your child. "You sure have fun with your dad. You and he laugh a lot." Or "You and your mom have a special relationship. She's a really good listener, isn't she?" Remember, **you don't have to like everything about the person to make a positive comment about the person.** You don't have to hate everything about the person you've divorced either. Even if you're resentful about the person's actions toward you, separate those actions out and pretend you're putting them in a mental "box" to take out and examine from time to time. Use another mental box for placing the positive characteristics in. Use the contents of this second box when you're with your child. Not only is it valuable for your child to hear you compliment the other parent but your action will also strengthen the bond between you and your child. You'll show your child that you're on his or her side.

Keeping Your Child Out of The Middle

It is not only the parents who place the child in the middle of parental confrontations. Children will consciously or unconsciously choose to place themselves in the middle of their parents' battles too. Therefore, it is important not to jump to the conclusion that the other parent is at fault for every situation. Your child may in fact be the manipulator. Your child may create a situation, such as a problem at school, which typically results in getting his parents talking. It is the child's attempt to reunite his parents. Sometimes the child takes a "middle" position because it has the power to get a parent upset. This is very empowering for a child; she learns to manipulate a situation just to see the expected result.

Example #1:

The child says, "Daddy said you're bad because you let me stay up late." If the parent responds with, "He did, did he?" and gets visibly angry and upset, the child discovers the enormous power he has, even when he's fabricated the situation.

Instead you can respond with, "It sounds like you're confused with the different bedtimes." This focuses the attention on the message about the problem rather than the inference about the other parent.

Example #2:

The child says, "Mommy says you don't love her anymore, but she still loves you."

How would you respond? Can you think of a way to respond that doesn't directly comment on the other parent's words, but focuses on the child's message?

Here's one way you could respond: "I don't love your mother like married people love each other. It seems as if you'd like us to get back together again. That is not going to happen. But you will still see both of us. We still love you very much."

Example #3:

The child says, "Daddy said you should spend more time with me and not go out with your friends."

Think of what you'd say.

_____

_____

_____

_____

Here's one way a parent could respond: "What do you think?" Based on your child's response, you could reflect the feeling. For instance, if the child says, "I would like you to spend more time with me," you could say something like, "It sounds like you would like more of my attention. What can we do together?" Then you can talk about the possible alternatives and agree on an acceptable solution.

Example #4:

The child says, "Mommy lets me have candy before dinner."

Maybe it's true; maybe not. It's better to **deal with the content of the message rather than focusing on the parent part of the message.** You might say, "At our house, our rules are different. We don't eat a snack right before dinner."

Sometimes the child is putting himself into the middle due to the anxiety of a loyalty bind. He is trying to keep both parents happy by telling them what he thinks they want to hear. The result is both parents are told distortions or non-truths.

What the Parent Can Do When the Child Is Manipulating

First it is important to remember that your child is not necessarily lying or trying to make trouble. Usually children are attempting to cope with the feeling of being caught in the middle. Therefore, this is not the time to discipline your child. Try the following:

1. Inform your child that you and the other parent have been talking. Tell them that you and the other parent are confused by things you are hearing. Encourage your child to tell both of you the same truth.

2. Use "we" language whenever possible when referring to the other parent. For example, if your child says "Daddy says you shouldn't help me with my homework," you might respond with something like, "Oh, thanks for telling me that. I will talk with your dad and <u>we</u> will get it straightened out."

3. Stay neutral and unemotional. Make sure you are not reinforcing your child's behaviors by overreacting.

Handling Difficult Moments
When You're on the Receiving End of a Note

You've decided that from now on you won't send a note or message for the other parent with your child. However, you receive a note from your co-parent which your child delivers to you. What should you do? Accept the note without reacting with words or actions. Review the note out of the presence of your child. Then contact the other parent during a time when your child will not overhear the conversation. Consider using an "I" message: "I'm concerned when Mary delivers a note from one of us to the other, she might feel responsible for our actions because it puts her in the middle. What I'd like is for you to contact me directly either by phone or mail."

When Children Refuse to Visit or Talk to a Parent

Another difficult moment that may tempt you to think the worst about the other parent arises when a child refuses to visit or talk to a parent. If you are that parent, it is easy to assume that the other parent may have done something to damage the relationship between you and your child; or if it's the other parent, that he or she has done something to the child.

However, the child's refusal may have nothing to do with you or the other parent. A young child may not want to leave the primary parent for fear that this parent may abandon her while she visits the other parent. This is a normal reaction. A child may refuse to speak to a parent on the phone because he is absorbed in his favorite game or watching his favorite television show. Always respect your child's desire to get off the phone. Likewise, a teenager may refuse to visit a parent because she'd rather be with her friends for the weekend. Remember, these situations occur in intact families as well. They do not necessarily have anything to do with the other parent's behavior.

When in doubt, check it out. And don't take it personally. Discuss the matter with the child's other parent, if possible. Ask the other parent if he or she has noticed the child's resistant behavior. What sense do they make of it? How long does the crying last? What usually stops the crying? What is the parent's response when the child becomes tearful or resistant? Mutually decide on a plan that will ease the transition. For example, if the child is young and anxious about being away, let her take her stuffed animal or doll along. Have the parent cover the doll with kisses and hugs before leaving. Then the young child can be encouraged to get lots of hugs and kisses whenever she wants them.

If the child refuses to speak to the parent on the phone, first review the situation and take into consideration your child's developmental level, interests and schedule. Agree on a time to call your child that would fit into both of your schedules. Know your child's activities and favorite television shows so you can avoid calling at those times. Remember that a young child's attention span is very short. Perhaps ask the child to sing one of his favorite songs or recite a nursery rhyme. If the child is in grade school, talk about friends at school, school projects and activities that you've shared. Have a routine for starting and finishing the conversation that the child can look forward to.

Ask a teenager's opinion about something—for example, a purchase you're considering, or a recent news topic. Try listening without giving your own opinion. Just say, "That's interesting. I hadn't looked at it that way. Do your friends think like you do about this issue?" If a teen is already on the phone with a friend when you call, he probably won't make time to talk to you. Try having him return the call when he's free; if he doesn't remember, don't take it personally. Remember, he is a teenager and not just the son of the other parent.

Don't Burden Your Child With Your Needs

You are hurting and you want to be honest. Your child is the only one around and is a willing listener. You're lonely without your former spouse. You're worried about the bills. You're afraid of the future. You're concerned with how the divorce will affect your child's life. You're nervous about starting to date again. So it is natural that you are tempted to share your deepest emotional concerns with your child. **STOP.**

You do have a right to experience, understand and release your own feelings. You do need support during this difficult time. You are human and you have emotional needs that require fulfillment. You need a place where you can receive the support you need. However your child is not the place. Please, call your friends. Make new friends. Go to support groups for parents who are divorced. Attend singles functions. Talk to your clergy. Contact family members with the greatest ability to listen. Make an appointment with a therapist. Go to the local mental health center. Please, please do reach out and obtain the emotional support you need at this time. **But do not depend on your child for fulfilling your emotional needs.**

Your child is already dealing with his own emotional turmoil. He is experiencing his own grief from the breakup of his family. She is grieving over the loss of her parent. He is worried about what his friends will think. She is concerned that her non-custodial parent doesn't love her anymore. He is unsure how to talk to his father's new partner or his mother's new partner. She is unclear where her loyalties lie. He is torn between wanting to love both parents and feeling like a traitor every time he shows his love. Your child cannot handle your additional burdens. This is too much to ask.

Your child may seem like he's not hurting; she may appear to "have it all together." But it's just as likely that he looks invulnerable but feels crushed inside. She can appear to be unaffected by all this fuss and yet be barely able to hold it together on the inside. Don't be fooled by appearances. Your children need to have the opportunity to be children, preparing themselves for handling adult concerns later on. Some children who are burdened with adult emotional responsibilities early in life are hugely affected throughout their lives. Don't take this emotional risk with your child.

The worst kind of emotional burden placed on a child is when one parent takes the role of the victim. This parent says things like, "I'm so lonely when you're not here," and "Your mother got everything, son; I'm left with nothing." The victim is putting the child in the middle through the use of guilt, effectively saying that it's all the other parent's fault. The other parent should feel guilty for doing that to "poor me." The child, of course, feels guilty by association.

Remember children do not separate themselves from their parents. Therefore, if one parent plays the role of victim, the child is at risk of feeling responsible for the victim-parent's feelings. The child is put in the unfortunate position of fulfilling the parent's emotional needs. He's gone from being a child to being the parent of his parent. It is too great a responsibility and he can break under the weight of its burden. On the other hand, if one parent is aggressive and the child views her as "bad," then the child is "bad" too. Instead, utilize your support system for fulfilling emotional needs and then set to work to improve the situation that is causing your greatest concerns. Put all your efforts into improving your financial position, making new social contacts and enjoying contact with your child. Share the best of your emotional experiences with your child and get help for handling negative emotional experiences. Your child will be the beneficiary of your wise decisions.

Tips For Easing Transitions

Traveling between homes may be difficult for your children. Each transition requires your children to make several adjustments. Although they may be anticipating being with their other parent, they may also experience some sadness about leaving you. When they leave the other parent, they may experience the same emotions once again. Comings and goings require your child to say hello and good-bye several times within a brief period of time.

1. Prepare for departure:

a. Talk to your child about what will happen while he is visiting with his other parent. Tell the other parent the reason you are asking for this information. Do the same for the other parent so she may be able to prepare your child in the same fashion. Say to your child, "Mommy is going to take you to the library."

b. Establish and maintain a routine. Before your child leaves for the other home, read a book, play a game or watch a short video together.

c. Establish and maintain a "good-bye" ritual. For example, give your child three kisses and a hug at each departure and say, "See you soon. Love you forever."

d. Pack a "comfort bag." Your child may want to transport favorite items such as a stuffed animal, a blanket, a book or an item that reminds him of the absent parent. Place a note or card in the bag for your child to discover at a later time.

2. During the transition:

a. Have your child adequately prepared and ready to leave on time. If you are transporting your child, be on time for dropping off and picking up.

b. Be courteous to the child's other parent. Avoid arguments and exchanging extraneous information. Do not send messages to the other parent through your child.

c. If your child is taking medication, be sure to transfer this medication and provide adequate instructions for how it is to be administered.

d. Consider a neutral exchange site if you or the other parent have difficulty refraining from arguing or trading insults in front of your child. Your child's day care or school can provide a neutral site.

e. Your child may have difficulty separating from one or both parents. Establishing rituals for departure and arrival will ease some of the anxiety.

3. Prepare for return:

a. Recognize that your child may need some time to be alone after returning home. Allow them to spend quiet time alone if they choose.

b. Establish and maintain a "hello" ritual. Once your child has unwound from his arrival, play a game, read a book, watch a favorite video or bake cookies.

c. Recognize that your child may not want to talk about the time spent with their other parent. Honor this preference.

During the transition process, acknowledge your child's feelings. Encourage her to talk about her feelings, but do not pressure her to talk.

Creating Two Homes

It is important to create a home environment that provides your child with a sense of belonging. Remember your child has two homes no matter how much time they spend in each.

1. Build predictability and security in both households:

a. Establish and maintain consistent routines and structure. Share routines that work with the other parent. As much as possible agree on bedtime, chores, morning rituals and homework. It will help both families.

b. Establish and maintain consistent rules and procedures for discipline. Although children can adapt to different rules and procedures in several settings, adhering to the same procedures eases their adjustment. Work together as a team whenever possible.

c. Establish and maintain responsibilities for your child. Children achieve a sense of belonging and build self-confidence by contributing to the family. Chores suited to your child's developmental level and interests can help her gain a sense of place in the family. Refer to the book "*Raising A Responsible Child*" by Elizabeth Ellis, Ph.D. for additional information.

d. Make time with your child as natural as possible. Sometimes the non-custodial parent tries to make up for time lost by filling weekends with "special events." What your child will remember most is the accumulation of experiences. Being there for bedtime, homework and pleasurable activities such as playing catch and reading books is important.

e. Spend one-on-one time with each of your children. Plan an activity that your child finds enjoyable. Remember it can be as simple as coloring, reciting nursery rhymes or putting puzzles together. This is especially important if you have a significant other.

f. Encourage your child to make friends in both neighborhoods and invite friends over.

2. Build continuity in both households:

a. Make a personal place for your child. It is important for her to have her own bed or at least a sleeping bag at each house. If she is unable to have her own room, provide a dresser drawer for her to store personal belongings.

b. Provide toilet articles and adequate changes of clothes including shoes, socks, pajamas and undergarments at each house.

c. Honor your child's preference if he wants to carry favorite items back and forth between homes.

d. Allow your child to contact the other parent by telephone each day. Establish a regularly scheduled time for telephone contact. Assure you child privacy. Avoid calling right before bedtime or during your child's favorite television show.

e. Allow your child to have a picture of the other parent in both homes. Allow your child to choose where the photograph will be located.

f. Post a calendar illustrating the days your child will be living with each parent.

g. Share important information with your child's other parent. Keep them informed of medical and dental visits and recommendations. Provide copies of report cards, school pictures and photographs of special events. Also, notify the other parent of important events in your child's life, such as school performances, sports activities and dance recitals, as soon as possible.

Truth or Consequences
Ways I Create a Loyalty Bind for My Child

Directions: It is time to take the lead and **own up to the truth** about your behaviors. Read the following and identify ALL the behaviors you have chosen. Remember children experience a loyalty bind whenever they are placed in the middle of their parents' conflict. This will make them feel uncomfortable loving both of you. Put an X on the number that indicates a behavior you have exhibited in the past, but you no longer do. Circle the number that indicates those behaviors you are currently choosing to do that hurt your child.

1. I make negative comments about the other parent.

2. I use negative body language or tone when referring to my child's other parent.

3. I allow relatives or friends to make negative comments when my child can overhear.

4. I ignore my child's presence while arguing with the other parent.

5. I discuss the character defects of the other parent when my child can overhear. This includes sharing information that will cause my child to see their other parent in a negative light—telling about an affair or a drug problem, for example. (Even if it is true, truth is not the issue, good parenting is.)

6. I stress to my children how much I miss them when they are with their other parent.

7. I ask my child questions about the visit with the other parent. I also ask questions about the parent, their relatives or someone my child cares for.

8. I say negative things about someone my child cares for.

9. I discuss child support or the lack of money with my child.

10. I discuss legal or other adult information with my child.

11. I ask my child to do things that might feel like spying.

12. I ask my child to keep secrets that might feel like spying.

13. I blame the other parent for our divorce or any other circumstances.

14. I refuse to allow the other parent to step into our home. I will not let my child bring his other parent in our home to see his room or into the backyard to see the new swing set.

15. At our child's activities, I refuse to sit on the same row with the other parent.

16. I refuse to speak or to make eye contact with the other parent.

17. I refuse to let my child take important items to her other home to show her other parent.

18. I imply that I am the better parent.

19. I make my child think I am a victim because of the actions of the other parent.

20. I send child support checks, letters or verbal messages through my child.

21. I make my child feel responsible for my emotional needs. I let my child take care of me.

22. I imply that my child is not safe in some way when she is with the other parent.

23. I refuse to let my child sit with his other parent at joint activities when he has come with me to the activity.

24. I block my child's contact with the other parent (phone calls, visits, etc.) or use screening methods to avoid their calls.

25. I remind my child that they can choose to live with me when they reach the legal age.

Loyalty Binds
What Can I Do Differently?

Directions: Using the previous activity sheet, complete the following exercise. Think about what you can do differently for each behavior that you circled on the previous page. Remember that your goal is not to protect the other parent, but to keep your child out of the middle. **Whenever you put the other parent down in any way, you are actively choosing to HURT your own child!**

My Behavior

What Can I Choose To Do Differently?

Please help
get your
child
out
of the
middle!

Loyalty Bind Prevention

I admit that I have allowed my anger and my hurt to interfere with good parenting. I now understand that some of my behaviors have been selfish and damaging to my child. This is difficult to admit and it causes me pain. However, I am committed to being a good parent even when it requires difficult impulse control, hard work and maturity. No matter how I feel about

_____ or _____ ,
(Name of other parent)   *(Name or relative or significant other)*

I will remember that both parents are important and loved by my child. I will honor my child's relationship with the other parent at any emotional expense to myself. My current and future decisions will reflect good parenting. As of this moment, I will give up the following destructive behaviors:

_____

_____

_____

_____

_____

_____

_____

_____

_____

_____

_____

_____

_____

_____

I will also encourage my child to let me know if and when I do any of the above behaviors. When given feedback I will **STOP** immediately and apologize to my child.

_____

Signature of a loving parent

Allowing My Child to Love
Both Families

Directions: Plan to do two or more of the following behaviors during the week. Add behaviors until you have practiced all ten.

1. Allow your child to spend time with extended family members on both sides of the family

2. Leave a framed pictures out of your child with both sets of their grandparents or extended family members.

3. Mention positive qualities of members of your child's extended family. Find a way to value what they have to offer to your child.

4. Recognize and comment on qualities that your child received from extended family members. Such as, "You have Grandpa's talent for drawing."

5. Encourage your child to remember the extended family member's birthdays, anniversaries, and other holidays with cards or phone calls.

6. Make sure your child responds appropriately when gifts are sent from the extended family.

7. If the extended family calls to speak to your child, and you answer the phone, attempt to say a few pleasant words. Remember, your child is listening.

8. Separate your negative feelings about your former spouse from your feelings for his/her family.

9. Do not assume that the extended family is speaking negatively about you.

10. Correct any inappropriate comments that you may have said with regard to the extended family. You might say, "I used to be upset with them, but I'm not as upset anymore. It's getting better all the time."

Dear Mom and Dad,

Gee, thanks for clearing the air about my loving both of you. I don't like it when I am pulled in two directions. It really makes me anxious and I worry at night. I never want to hurt your feelings. I just want to love both of you.

Your torn child,

XXXXXXOOOOO

Chapter Two Review

1. What is the meaning of the Cooperative Parenting logo on the cover of this guide?

2. In what ways have you put your child into a loyalty bind in the past? What are you currently doing that might create a loyalty bind for your child?

3. How is your child's self-esteem connected to you and your child's other parent? How will negative comments, negative body language and avoidance affect your child's self-esteem?

4. Why is it so important to value your child's other parent?

5. What are some things you can do to encourage your child to love both parents?

6. When your child shares information about his other parent that is upsetting to you, how should you respond?

7. When should you use "we" language, and why is it important?

8. Why is it inappropriate to get emotional support from your child?

9. What have you done to ease your child's adjustment to two homes?

10. Why is it important for your child to stay in contact with both sides of the family? How would this apply to former step siblings?

3.

Letting Go Or Holding On
Changing My Long Term Role

3.

Letting Go or Holding On
(Changing My Long Term Role)

In the last two chapters, the focus was on the children of divorced parents. In the next two chapters, the focus is on you, the parents of those children. The information here will help you make an important choice in your life: to have a new co-parenting relationship with your child's other parent or to hold on to the past. What you decide reflects your view of your role following the divorce.

In this first section we'll look at three roles you play in life and their differences before and after divorce: 1) your personal role as a single person or member of a married couple; 2) your role as a member of a family; and 3) your role as a parent. Then we'll see how a person lets go of the old role in order to "realign" in the new role. Finally we'll see what prevents realignment from occurring and what you can do to ensure a smooth transition in your own life. Although the focus is on you, we won't ignore the impact that the adjustment to your new roles has on your children. Because of them you are open to new information which could bring you and your children more happiness.

Your Changing Role

Over a lifetime people play many roles. For example, you are a parent to your children, a child to your parents, and a confidant to your friends. In this section we're going to focus on three of your current roles and the structure of each.

Personal Status (Single, Married)

Your personal status has changed at least three times in your lifetime thus far. First you were Single, then your status changed to Married, and after your divorce, it changed again to Single. A simple diagram of these structures might look like this:

During each of these periods in your life, certain functions or needs, such as financial needs and social needs, had to be carried out or fulfilled. A list of these functions appears in the left column of the chart entitled Chart of Responsibilities.

CHART OF RESPONSIBILITIES

Single (Before Marriage)	**Married**	**Single** (After Divorce)

Functions: Financial needs Social needs Sexual needs Emotional needs Housekeeping needs (chores) Friendship/companionship needs		

Individual Role:

Now that you are single you are responsible for all the above, not your former spouse. Likewise, it is your former spouse's responsibility to resolve his or her own needs. You are responsible for your financial future, for obtaining emotional support, for handling the daily housekeeping chores and for ensuring your own social life.

The person responsible is the one who makes the decisions and is accountable for the results. In some ways, it's similar to having an acquaintance. You don't give an acquaintance your advice on how he uses his time or what she does with her money. And you would not pry into their personal business. Your acquaintance is the one who is accountable for making his or her own decisions.

Parenting Role:

Of course, there is a difference between this example and your own situation because your former spouse is also the parent of your child(ren). And that does complicate the issue. If there were no children involved, you might not continue the relationship with your former spouse at all. Because there are children involved, you do need a continued relationship. However, the areas of shared responsibility are limited to those involving the children. In all the other areas listed in the chart, your relationship with your former spouse is like that with any other acquaintance. Each of you has completely separate responsibilities in those matters. It is only in the role of parents that some responsibilities are still shared.

Let's focus on the parenting role now. On the next page is the Child-Rearing Decisions Activity. Read the directions and complete the activity now.

Child-Rearing Decisions Activity

Directions: In the space below, list ten of the decisions you make about your child's life when he/she is with you. Think about daily care, discipline, health issues, school, etc.

1. _____

2. _____

3. _____

4. _____

5. _____

6. _____

7. _____

8. _____

9. _____

10. _____

Now read over your list and put a check by those items that your child's other parent makes when your child is with him or her.

In this activity, you saw how each parent makes decisions about the welfare of your child independently. You no longer confer with your child's other parent about the minor decisions which affect your child. But as the diagram below shows, some decisions are still made by both parents.

Married With Children   Single (Divorced) With Children

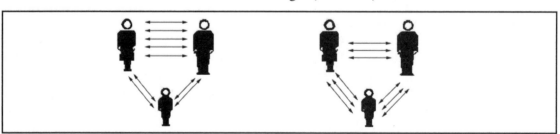

The diagram on the left shows the relationship between the parents and a child during the marriage. The diagram on the right shows the relationship between the parents and the child after the divorce.

The lines indicate how decisions about child-rearing are made. The line between the parents refers to decisions made by the parents together while the lines down the sides indicate decisions that are made independently (for example, those items on the list you've just completed in the Child-Rearing Decisions Activity). Although the number of decisions made together and those made separately may differ from those made prior the divorce, the most important fact is that there are still decisions that need to be made together.

Therefore, it is extremely important that, after divorce, parents have an ongoing relationship with one another.

In the best interests of the child, parents must continue to parent together even though they choose no longer to live together. The relationship between the two parents must become realigned into a different structure. With a new alignment between the parents, a new term for parents after divorce is also needed. We use the term "co-parents" to designate parents following a divorce.

Family Role:

The third role that is important in our discussion is your role as a member of the family. Below is a diagram of a family both before and after the divorce. The diagram on the left is a drawing of a family with one child prior to the divorce. The diagram on the right is a drawing of the child's family after the divorce. The main difference is that the child now has two houses.

Circle your current family. You probably circled yourself and your children (and drew in any new members of your family if you have remarried). Your child's family consists of the same people as before but in two different locations. It's important that both you and your child have a picture of the family after the divorce. Some people have a misconception that a non-custodial parent no longer has a family. Even if the location has changed, your role in the family is still vitally important. Your child has two homes.

In this section we've discussed three important roles you have in your current life: your personal role, your role as a parent, and your role as a member of a family. Although the responsibilities may have changed in each role, all three continue to be an important part of your life.

Letting Go

On paper, the redrawing of roles looks pretty simple. But it isn't simple, is it? It's much more complicated due to one element that isn't reflected in the drawings: Emotions, the stuff that makes us human.

As a matter of fact, because of the emotional turmoil involved, many people have compared divorce to death or to many deaths. In the space below write down a few of the ways that divorce is similar to death.

_____

_____

_____

_____

_____

Grieving

For most people, divorce is a very difficult transition. And surprisingly, this is true even for the person who initiated the divorce. In fact, most people grieve over the loss just like they do when a close relative dies. And it's not only the adults who grieve; the children mourn their losses just as deeply.

Children often mourn the loss of the family structure as they knew it and the loss of their dream of the perfect family. If they have moved, they mourn the loss of friends, their neighborhood, school and church. Their feelings of security have also been temporarily shattered.

Adults mourn some of those same things plus the loss of lifestyle, shared intimacy, economic security, friendship and companionship. They too mourn the loss of the dream of the perfect relationship and the dream of the perfect family life.

Stages of Grief

We often refer to the process of grieving as the "stages of grief," first described by Elizabeth Kubler-Ross and expanded upon by many other writers. As you read the brief description of each stage, write down any thoughts about your own experience that the description triggers for you. There is a place for you to make notes after each description.

Shock

This stage is often described by people as feeling completely numb. Some say they feel nothing, as though they were anesthetized. Some people notice a kind of panic that accompanies, precedes or follows the numbness. You may have a hard time concentrating or even expressing yourself when you are in this stage of grief.

_____

_____

_____

Denial

When people stubbornly refuse to grieve, they are said to be in denial. Since grief is painful, most people try to put it off at least temporarily. You might hear people say, "I don't care anyway," or "She was never there for me anyway." However, if denial continues, it may be impossible for the person to move on to healthier stages of life.

_____

_____

_____

Guilt

Feelings of guilt emerge when you examine what you might have done to cause the divorce or what you did do which may have hurt the other person. Your thoughts in this stage may have started with the phrase, "If only I . . ."

_____

_____

_____

Anger

Anger is often present during the grief process. Following divorce it may take the form of blaming the former spouse not only for initiating the divorce but also for destroying your dream of the perfect family and home. It may even be turned toward yourself for your inability to prevent the divorce.

_____

_____

_____

Bargaining/Depression

Grieving often brings feelings of isolation and loneliness; this is often the case in divorce. Almost as a last effort before resolving some of the grief is a last stand at bargaining with God, with oneself or with one's former partner. When that last big effort doesn't work, the person often experiences depression.

_____

_____

_____

Hope

The hope experienced here is different from The Hope Trap discussed in the next chapter. Here, it's part of the resolution process that indicates hopefulness for the future. It's a start on the road to the future, leaving the worst behind you.

Acceptance

In this final stage sadness is felt but it is shared with an acceptance that there is no going back. Acceptance does not deny the pain of the experience nor the joy of past experiences. Instead it accepts the present as the only alternative and leaves you ready to face the future.

Have you experienced each of these stages? You may experience them in a different order from the order in which they are listed here. You might return to one stage more than once. Does it seem like you're stuck in any stage? If so, you may need professional help to move on if you are to recover from the disruption of divorce.

Handling Memories

After divorce, many people have misconceptions about memories from the past. Some people mistakenly believe we have to give up everything about the past in order to begin focusing on the future. Others mistakenly believe that everything about the past should be erased if it isn't continuing. Or that everything about a past relationship is dirtied or ruined if the present relationship isn't a good one. These are all misconceptions.

The wonderful memories can remain wonderful. Those times did exist. The picnic, the party, the intimacy, the shared experience, were all real. They are as much a part of your history as your child's first step or first word. You can still treasure them. The fact that your situation is different now does not alter them.

Memory Activity

In the space below, write down one or two <u>positive memories</u> that you want to treasure that include your former spouse. These memories are uniquely yours forever.

Memories (including you and former spouse)

_____

_____

_____

_____

Memories (Including you, your former spouse and child/ren)

_____

_____

_____

_____

You may be sad that you won't share these experiences again. However, no experience can be duplicated. You can still treasure the good moments and appreciate them for being a part of your life.

Remembering the positive times can assist you and your child with the grieving process. Many of those who refuse to remember the good times are often the same ones who will refuse to accept and heal from the divorce.

Although you may not be ready to fully accept the divorce or your new life, you may find that forgiveness can also be an additional healing tool for you in this process.

Forgiveness:

The concept of forgiveness can be very disturbing when someone has been seriously hurt. Yet the ability to forgive can help you let go of pain. When a parent will not let go of a belief that they were not loved, or that they cannot trust the other parent, they imprison themselves and their child to a future of pain.

Getting a divorce is painful enough on your child. Conflict and tension between you and your co-parent will negatively impact your child's self esteem. Therefore, to reduce conflict, reduce tension, and to let go of old pain, consider forgiveness. If you will not, your anger, your hurt and your pain will go on indefinitely. This doesn't sound like much fun! What do you have to lose? Pain?

Forgiveness Does Not Mean:

- That you condone the co-parent's behavior.
- Your pain is not real or not justified.
- You have to receive an apology or mutual recognition.
- A reconciliation.

It will, however, help your family work better.

According to Ron Classes, the co-director of the Center For Peacemaking and Conflict Studies at Fresno Pacific University, "Forgiveness is the process of making things as right as possible."

Sometimes forgiveness is granted after a confrontation followed by an apology. Experiencing the other person's remorse helps us let go of the unforgivable act. We desperately want the other person to accept responsibility for what they have done to us. When they are unwilling or unable to offer an apology, or when an apology may not be possible at the moment (when your child is in the room), you can still choose to forgive rather than seek revenge. There are many ways to encourage this process.

One ritual involves writing an honest letter to your former spouse to release the unforgivable pain. It is just as useful, and usually more productive, to write the letter and destroy it. Giving it to your former spouse may create additional problems for you or your child. And, by all means, do not share this letter with your child or place it somewhere where they may find it.

No matter what your religious beliefs might be, you can use forgiveness as a powerful tool to heal yourself. This in turn will help heal your child.

> - Forgiveness can do more for the person who is forgiving than for the individual who is being forgiven.
> - Forgiveness has the potential for healing the damaged past.
> - Forgiveness is a decision, a choice.

The Cost Of Holding On:

- Attempting to be appropriate with the co-parent, especially under pressure, will drain a tremendous amount of your energy.
- Old pain will blur your vision in the next potential relationship.
- It will eat away at your health and interfere with your sleep.
- It will also eat away at your self-esteem.

The Cost To Your Child:

The most obvious cost will be that you and the other parent will be in conflict. You will become stirred up in the presence of the co-parent, maybe even by the sound of his or her name. Even if you are committed to not being negative towards your child's other parent, you will nonetheless create significant stress for your child. Children are like radar; they can read us a mile away. Your words may be appropriate but your body tension will scream negative messages about the other parent.

Consider this: If your message implies that the other parent is "no good!" your child will have to do one of the following:

Your Child Will:

- Agree with you and develop an impaired relationship with the other parent.
- Agree with you now but resent you and your message later.
- Disagree with you and defend the other parent.
- Minimize their own needs in order to be equally connected to both of you.

Any and all of these choices will damage your child's fragile sense of self. Both parents are essential to your child's healthy development.

Disengaging

The Necessity of Disengaging

Grieving is part of the process of letting go of the old role and adapting to the new one. What would happen if someone didn't let go of the old role? Let's take an extreme example: What would happen if a person's spouse died and the survivor put all his or her attention on the loss of the loved one? That person would be stuck, unable to cope with things around him or her.

It would be like being caught in quicksand. And if that person has children, the children would also be caught in turmoil.

"Letting go" of a divorced spouse is just as important as the letting go of a deceased spouse. Despite the pain of making the transition, it is necessary to let go of the old relationship if a person is to thrive. It is imperative for the children too.

Advantages of Disengaging

The word we use for letting go of the marital relationship after a divorce is **"disengaging."** You might think of it as detaching from the former spouse. Think of the words or phrases that come to mind when you think of being *attached* to a person and write them below. Then think of all the words and phrases that come to mind when you think of being *detached* and write them on the second group of lines below.

Describe what it means to be "ATTACHED" to someone:

_____

_____

_____

Describe what it means to be 'DETACHED" from someone:

_____

_____

_____

Although we often think of the emotional pain involved, detaching or disengaging from the former spouse also has advantages. The person can begin to enjoy life again; he can start focusing on the future instead of the past; she can start making decisions that improve her situation. They take more responsibility for themselves.

Ways that People Stay Engaged

Despite the value of disengaging, the pain and fear of transition is so great for some people that they put their efforts into staying attached or engaged instead. There are many ways to do that. For example, one person continues handling the car repairs for the other or continues cooking for the other person. Another prepares his former spouse's taxes; another mows the lawn. These are all ways that someone stays engaged with a former spouse.

Individuals use a variety of excuses for these behaviors. They say things like, "I was trying to save her money," or "I wanted to make sure he was getting some nutrition." These examples are all ways that people stay engaged physically.

They also stay engaged emotionally or psychologically. This type of attachment is extremely strong but it is harder for most people to detect. A spouse may stay negatively attached through emotions such as anger and bitterness. Below are two examples of couples who are emotionally engaged with their former spouse.

Engaged Through Revenge

Barbara and Bill have been divorced for three years. They have two children. When Bill comes to pick up the children, Barbara won't let him in until the clock is exactly at 6 PM. As soon as he enters the room he starts calling her a witch. She retaliates with "the jerk that left me and the kids destitute."

Out of sight of one another, the two continue their lifelong battle. The children hear about "the dummy I was married to" and about "the airhead that I used to live with." Bill buys clothes for the children that he knows Barbara hates. She gets the kids haircuts that she knows Bill will despise. Bill doesn't tell Barbara how the children got the cuts and bruises on their knees when they fell off their bikes; Barbara doesn't tell Bill the time of the softball games that the children play. Bill tells the children how much he misses them and how their mother won't let him see them more often. Barbara has taken Bill to court twice to get higher child support payments. Bill sold one of his cars for much less than it was worth so that Barbara would get less of the money; Barbara retaliated by selling off the paintings that his former students from his art class had given him.

Emotionally, these two people are still bound to one another. It's like having a rope tied between them. When one pulls on it, it causes the other to be jerked in response. Then that other one retaliates by jerking on the rope causing the first person to be pulled toward him/her. And the cycle continues. Each person chooses actions for the sole purpose of getting a reaction from the other. The focus becomes **hurting the other person rather than getting on with one's own life.**

There's an old familiar quote that says, "Bitterness binds you to each other as tightly as your love once did." The couple into revenge shows you an example of how bitterness ties the two people together in a <u>never-ending</u> knot.

Harmful to Children

Being *Engaged Through Revenge* clearly shows how staying engaged is harmful to the children. Decisions made by the parents don't take the children's needs into consideration. They take actions not because they are right for the children but because they are wrong for the other parent. The children get put in the middle and are used for the purpose of creating tension in the other parent (even though the children must then live with the result of that tension). Although staying engaged causes significant problems to the parent, it causes even greater problems for the children. After all, the children don't have a choice. They're also tied to the rope with no control of their own.

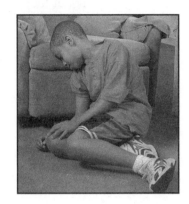

Let's look at another example of emotional engagement.

Engaged Through Hope

> *Steve and Cindy have been divorced a year. Cindy initiated the divorce. Steve still believes that Cindy is the only person who can make his dreams come true. Steve plans his weekend around places Cindy might frequent so that he might run into her. He makes a special effort to find something about their young child he has to tell Cindy about so that he can spend more time with her. He volunteers to babysit when Cindy works out of town on work assignments so that he can see her more often. He frequently tells her how miserable he is without her, hoping this will bring her back to him. He tells his small child that when Mommy and Daddy get back together she will have a family again.*

This couple, too, is still engaged. Steve's life revolves around Cindy. He makes decisions based not on the needs of the child, but on the opportunity of staying engaged with his former spouse. This prevents him from establishing a new life for himself and it puts the child in jeopardy of emotional trauma. It turns the child into a pawn used for satisfying the parent's needs. It puts the child's needs last.

If you sympathize with Steve, you probably experienced similar emotions soon after the divorce. However, if you're locked into these behaviors a year or so later, it's very important for you and your child(ren) that you let go of this unhealthy bind.

Staying in Limbo

Breaking with the past role is important when developing a future role. If people stay attached to their former spouse either through anger and conflict or hope, it keeps them in a state of limbo. It's neither the role or relationship that came before the divorce and it isn't a role or relationship that can guide the person into the future.

People stay in limbo for many reasons. The first is fear. Staying engaged may mean there's lots of conflict, but at least it's familiar. Letting go and moving on to the future is scary. It's the unknown and one doesn't know what to expect.

Another reason people stay engaged is the refusal to give up their dreams. Like Steve, they wanted a perfect marriage and a perfect family. Letting go means having to accept the death of those dreams.

Assumptions about how parents are supposed to act when they're divorced and expectations about their role are two additional obstacles to disengaging. We will explore these problems and offer solutions later in this chapter.

Letting Go

Making the Decision to Let Go

For most people, the first step in healing from the wounds of divorce is to make the decision to let go of the past. Remember the squirrel we talked about in the first chapter? This step, too, requires a leap of faith. You have to give up holding onto the past in order to get something better for the future. Have you made that decision? Was there a specific point in your life when you decided it's time to move on? When you thought that the future has got to get better than this? When you decided if it's to happen, it's up to you to make it happen? When you decided to look forward rather than looking back? If you have not yet made that decision, isn't it about time you did?

On the spaces provided below write what it would mean for you if you really let go.

Making the Decision to Let Go

_____

_____

_____

_____

_____

A Temporary Clean Cut

Staying engaged is so damaging that sometimes it's better to make a clean cut from one's former spouse. A clean cut means not seeing the former spouse (even making transitions with the child at the child-care center or school to avoid contact). It means not speaking to the other person (leaving messages on the person's answering machine when you know that he/she won't be at home). It means removing all evidence of the person so as not to be reminded of him/her (except for pictures in the child's room).

This solution would be damaging to the children if it continued beyond a few months. But as a temporary measure, enabling a parent to disengage, it can be valuable. How do you know?

If the amount of conflict between the parents is so high that every contact breeds increased tension, then a clean cut is in order. But remember, in the interests of the children, it must be temporary.

Letting Go Physically

Do you remember some of the examples for how people stay engaged physically? Now we'll concentrate on *letting go*, physically. That means no longer mowing the former spouse's lawn, making their dinner, or balancing their checkbook. It means allowing the former spouse to take responsibility for him/herself.

It may seem harsh or cold. Yet it is important to let go and allow your former spouse to let go of you.

Letting Go Emotionally

Disengaging emotionally is usually harder than disengaging physically. It means no longer expecting emotional support, social support or even friendship from one's former spouse. It means getting one's own emotional needs met elsewhere and not taking responsibility for his or her emotional needs. Disengaging means detaching from the former spouse. It means refusing to make decisions based on his opinions, no longer sharing intimate thoughts with her, and not allowing the person to push your emotional buttons. It means refraining from using the child to seek vengeance. It means cutting the cords that bind you to one another and letting go of the bitterness that keeps you entwined.

Rituals for Letting Go

Marriage begins with the marriage ceremony. It formalizes the relationship and gives it a starting point. One reason that divorce is so difficult is because there is no symbolic ceremony or ritual to mark the transition point. You might be surprised to find that creating your own ritual or ceremony can be helpful for letting go of the former relationship and for beginning a new relationship with one's former spouse. One such ceremony is The Candle Ritual.

The Candle Ritual

In this ceremony, you light a single candle symbolizing your new independent life. Then as you hold your single candle, you visualize this candle lighting your way to a future filled with bright happiness. You allow this candle to be your guide as you create your own future. You decide to keep this candle lit within you even after the candle itself is extinguished. Decide to extinguish the candle when you are ready to let go and blow out the candle.

The Rock Ritual

A second ritual involves a little more creativity. Go out and find a large stone or rock. It should be heavy enough to provide some weight but not so heavy that you can't carry it around with you. The rock symbolizes the burden you carry when you're still attached to your former spouse. Put it in your purse or pocket for several days. Be aware of it dragging you down as you carry it from place to place. Feel how cumbersome it is and how it interferes with your easy movement. Think how pleasant it would be to no longer have to carry it with you everywhere. Keep it with you a little longer.

When you get to the point that you're ready to leave the rock behind, think carefully of all the advantages of no longer being burdened by this weight. Think about how it is up to you to remove the rock from your pocket or purse and decide to leave it behind. Although you've gotten used to carrying this extra weight around (you may even miss its familiar presence when it's gone), you've decided to put it aside and allow yourself to move freely onto the next stage in you life. Put the rock in a place where you won't see it anymore. Leave it behind or bury it in the ground. Let yourself feel the renewed energy you have now that you no longer have to carry the burden with you.

Marriage Certificate Ritual

On page 65 you will find a Marriage Certificate. You may want to make a copy of your real certificate or fill in information on the one we have provided. Some options for your ritual could be 1) bury it; 2) burn it; or 3) cut it into small strips and put it into a balloon. Then say goodbye and let the balloon go. Be creative.

The Dis-engagement Contract

A fourth ritual can be carried out by reading and completing the Dis-engagement Contract on the next page. When two people make the commitment to marry, we often say that they're engaged. When the decision is made to let go of that marriage bond, we call it "disengaged." This contract will help you make that new commitment in your life.

Disengagement Contract

My Name is _____, and I married _____
         (Your Name)   *(Former Spouse's Name)*

on _____. Our children are _____.
   (Date of Wedding)   *(Child/ren's Name)*

Our marriage ended on _____. Therefore, _____
                      (Date of Divorce)   *(Co-Parent's Name)*

is no longer my partner or my lover. We are both free to choose new partners. We are no longer connected by love and desire. We are only, and forever, connected through our child/ren. We may not always agree, but we choose to work together cooperatively. We will need to see each other with new eyes, eyes of caring parents only. We will work very hard to let go of the past and to start fresh to parent together. We owe this to our child/ren.

When we were married, we maintained two roles, that of parent and spouse. Now we will let go of the married role and focus only on a parenting role. This severing must be complete and clean. Remnants of the past are my responsibility to release.

I am responsible for me. I have custody of myself and I can choose to be bitter or choose to be better in the future. I am choosing to be strong for our child/ren. I choose to make mature decisions, not emotional decisions for the sake of our child/ren. I will control the impulse to say negative things about my co-parent when my child may be able to overhear me. I will learn to separate my feelings of the co-parent from my child's feelings. I will separate my needs from my child/ren's needs and I will allow them all the room they need to love _____.
                                                          (My Child's Other Parent)

I am committed to being a good parent even when it hurts.

Parent Signature _____ Date _____

EMOTIONS LOG
1 (mild intensity) - 5 (high intensity)

Directions: Keep track of the times you are emotionally upset (positive or negative feelings) with your child's other parent. Keep a diary or list on this page. Be sure to rate the intensity of your emotions.

Date	Emotion	Rating	Impact on your child

EMOTIONS LOG *(continuation)*

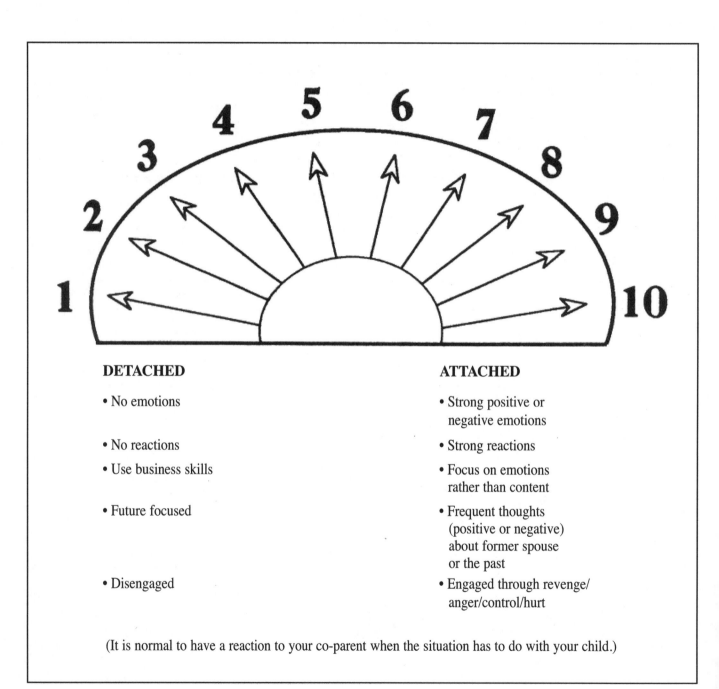

ATTACHMENT SCALE

Directions: Consider the degree of the emotions you feel for your former spouse, both positive and negative. Now, honestly mark the scale to show the degree of attachment you still have for him or her. Remember, if you are bitter, revengeful, angry, distrusting, dependent (just to name a few) you are still emotionally attached to your co-parent.

DETACHED

- No emotions

- No reactions
- Use business skills

- Future focused

- Disengaged

ATTACHED

- Strong positive or negative emotions

- Strong reactions

- Focus on emotions rather than content

- Frequent thoughts (positive or negative) about former spouse or the past

- Engaged through revenge/ anger/control/hurt

(It is normal to have a reaction to your co-parent when the situation has to do with your child.)

Marriage Certificate

It is certified that on the _____ **day of,** _____,

one thousand nine hundred _____

_____
(husband)

and

_____
(wife)

were United in Marriage

Dear Mom and Dad,

I guess if I have to get used to the idea that you two are no longer married, you should get used to it too. Maybe when all of us are used to this, it will get easier. The best news is that you two will <u>always</u> be my parents! Thanks.

Your hopeful child,
XXXXXOOOOOXXXXX

Chapter Three Review

1. What stages of grief have your experienced? Are you stuck in any stage? If so, what can you do to assist the healing process?

2. Are you able to remember the happy times between you and your former spouse? Why is this important to you? Why would this be important for your child? What positive memory have you shared with your child?

3. What is the cost of holding on to the negative emotions you have for your child's other parent? What is the cost for your child?

4. What are your child's options when he or she is forced to choose between their parents?

5. How attached are you to your child's other parent? What can you do to detach even more?

4.

Make It Better or Keep It Bitter

Choosing My Personal Path

Choosing My Personal Path
(Make it Better or Keep it Bitter)

The last chapter focused on the importance of letting go of the old marital relationship. Although this shift is difficult, particularly for the spouse who was "left," it is essential for you to see the former spouse as only your child's other parent. The only healthy way to survive is to let go of the old role and the emotions associated with it and begin your new role as co-parents.

This chapter will help you clarify your choices and help you identify the path you are on. Are you ready to move on by making it better or are you choosing to stay unhappy? It is your choice. Remember the path you choose will significantly affect your child's emotional future. Let's look at how the last chapter ties in with this one. Notice in the diagram below how letting go allows you to emotionally disengage. As you disengage, you are able to realign your relationship from former spouse to co-parent.

Letting Go $\longrightarrow$	**Disengage** $\longrightarrow$	**Realign**

Realignment

Letting go of one role implies that a new role will take its place. We've discussed the changing responsibilities of a person moving from the personal status "Married" to the personal status of "Single." We've also discussed how some aspects of this new relationship compare to the relationship with any other acquaintance. Now we need to look more closely at the role of the parent after divorce and the continuing relationship with the child's other parent.

Co-parent

The term we used to describe parents following divorce is "co-parents." You've heard the word co-chair before. It means equal in accountability although it may mean that the two individuals have different responsibilities. The term "co-parent" has the same implication: you have equal accountability for parenting but you differ in specific responsibilities. It also implies equal worth.

Purpose of Realignment

The only reason for a continued relationship after divorce is to ensure the best environment for bringing up your children. Therefore the new relationship between parents is built on the principle of addressing the needs of the children.

Working Relationship/Business Relationship

The new relationship between co-parents is often compared to a business or working relationship. In the space provided, list some of the characteristics of a good business or working relationship. What are the guidelines that make a business relationship work?

Characteristics of a Business Relationship

_____

_____

_____

_____

_____

_____

Guidelines for a Business Relationship

Although your list of the characteristics found in a good, working relationship may differ, there are likely to be similarities. See if your list includes any of these characteristics.

1. The individuals in a business relationship are dedicated to a common goal.

A business relationship often means working in partnership to fulfill a contract, meet an obligation or manufacture a product. It can also mean that the vendor and purchaser work together to meet their respective schedule and pricing needs. In all cases the relationship exists because there is a common purpose involved.

What's the common purpose in co-parenting? It's to raise children who are emotionally and physically healthy. Co-parents share this purpose and can work together to meet this common objective.

2. The individuals are committed to a win-win relationship.

If both participants are committed to a win-win relationship, the business relationship will continue for a long time. However, if either one of the parties moves toward a win-lose position—trying to gain the upper hand or take advantage of the other—the relationship will deteriorate or be broken off.

In co-parenting, there is a need for the continued long-term relationship between the parties in order to successfully parent the child. Therefore, the two parties will benefit from being committed to a win-win relationship. This means making an effort to meet the needs of both parties at all times. It means not looking for or taking advantage of short-term wins because of the likelihood of long-term damage. And that would have a detrimental effect on their ability to meet their long-term goal.

3. The individuals negotiate differences when they disagree or when new circumstances arise.

In any business relationship, changing circumstances arise. The price of raw materials changes, causing renewed negotiations in the price of the finished goods. Availability of resources causes changes in schedules; new requests must be factored into the budget and schedule. When these changes occur, the two parties must negotiate an acceptable solution. Sometimes this means renegotiation of terms or it means coming to a new agreement. A good faith effort is made to meet the needs of both parties and differences are resolved through win-win negotiation.

New circumstances and differences in opinion are sure to arise in a co-parent relationship. From time to time, your child's sports schedule or religious activities may conflict with pre-arranged time-sharing plans. Parents' job commitments may interfere with the children's schedules and time-sharing plans. As your children mature and grow, their needs and interests will change. When these changes occur, co-parents must negotiate acceptable solutions. Co-parents in a business relationship negotiate in good faith so that both are winners and the children never lose.

4. The relationship is limited to specific topics and objectives.

In any business relationship, only certain aspects of the business are put on the table for discussion. Other areas are out of bounds and would not enter into the relationship. For example, a purchaser and vendor may discuss the price of products and timing of scheduling, but not the qualifications of a new hire.

The same principle holds true for the new co-parent relationship. The areas of common discussion center on specific aspects of child-rearing. They do not encompass the dating patterns of the parties or even the financial decisions of either party (including how the custodial parent spends the child-support money). These topics are outside the boundaries of the new working relationship.

5. The individuals observe common courtesies.

Business relationships observe common courtesies such as calling to make appointments when there is something to be discussed, notifying the other party when there is a change in scheduling, keeping the other party current on issues that affect their common goal. Communication takes place during normal business hours or at times that are acceptable to both parties. The voice tones used are pleasant. Requests are made rather than demands and information is shared rather than hoarded.

Co-parents in business relationships also observe common courtesies. They too call to make an appointment when a topic needs to be discussed rather than catching the person at transition times. Co-parents notify the other party when there is a change that affects their common objective (such as something going on in the child's life at school) and they keep the other parent current on policies (such as the new schedule for sports practice or dance lessons). They share rather than hoard information, such as letting the other parent know about report card grades or appointments with school personnel. Voice tones are pleasant and requests are made rather than demands.

6. The individuals communicate with facts, not feelings.

In a business relationship, the two parties expect to have differences which they must negotiate. However, during the communication itself, feelings are put aside so that they do not interfere. It is understood that sarcasm, whining, demanding, placating, moralizing, advising and/or complaining will only reduce the chances of a satisfactory outcome to the discussion. Clear, unemotional communication that uses facts to move toward solutions to problems increases the chances for continuing a viable, long-term relationship.

In a realigned relationship, co-parents need to communicate with facts rather than feelings. Emotions tend to interfere with the problem-solving process and reduce the chances for a successful relationship. Since the co-parents are no longer responsible for emotional support, emotions should not play a part in their continued communication. When emotions are set aside, the two people can better work toward finding solutions to any outstanding problems.

> **Removing emotions from communication does not mean denying them. Find another time or place to express them safely where they will be less likely to negatively influence the co-parent relationship and your child.**

Check below indicating which of these business relationship skills you already use with the co-parent. Then place an X on the behaviors/skills you have not mastered.

1. _____ I work toward common goals with the co-parent.
2. _____ I work toward a win-win arrangement rather than for me to win.
3. _____ I use negotiation skills when attempting to resolve issues with the co-parent.
4. _____ I stay focused on addressing only one topic at a time.
5. _____ I treat the co-parent with respect and I demonstrate this by common courtesy.
6. _____ I am able to discuss details or concerns without becoming emotional.

Summary

Realignment for parents following divorce means forming a relationship that differs in structure from the old parenting relationship. The framework of a business relationship helps to define guidelines that work for this new structure. The realigned relationship limits the emotional involvement of the two parties. Instead a structure is established that allows the two parties to communicate about their child's welfare, solve problems, negotiate solutions and share valuable information so that both parents will realize their mutual goal of providing for the emotional well-being of the child.

Obstacles to Realignment

Assumptions

There are several obstacles to realignment. However, you can choose to assert your control over these obstacles. The first obstacle is the assumptions that adults bring to the process of divorce. Look at the following cartoon.

What assumptions does the cartoon illustrate? It shows the **adversarial position** underlying most adult thoughts about divorce.

Since divorce goes through legal channels, many people automatically assume that a divorce has to be adversarial. After all, think of the words you usually associate with court cases: winning and losing, court battles, court orders, pro and con, for and against, plaintiff and defendant. The words surrounding the legal process often influence adults to think of divorce more like a crime, with a good guy and a bad guy, one guilty party and one victim demanding punishment for the guilty party.

As a result, the parties in the divorce case start treating one another as adversaries, looking for a chance to punish the other for crimes against the marriage. When they assume they're supposed to act in a win-lose manner, they do act in a win-lose manner. However, it's not only the other parent who gets hurt in the process—the child in the middle takes the greatest hit. As parents escalate their conflict, the child is the one who is hurt even more.

STOP AND ASK YOURSELF . . .

If my child/ren were asked to complete the following sentence, how would they honestly answer?

My _____ is the good guy, and my _____ is the bad guy.

Have you contributed to this simplistic, black-and-white reasoning? If so, how?

_____

_____

_____

_____

_____

Has your explanation about the divorce reflected blame? If so, what can be done to correct this? For example: Create a simple "nonblaming" explanation.

_____

_____

_____

_____

_____

Expectations

Similar to assumptions are the adults' underlying expectations of each other. We all form expectations of others' behavior based on our observations of their actions in the past. However, those expectations get us in trouble when we don't allow them to change. It has been said that "the past does not necessarily equal the future." People do grow and change. Divorce sometimes causes those changes. So if, years after the divorce, one parent still thinks of the other as dependent, verbally abusive or uninvolved with their own children, they might be wrong. And they could send the wrong message to their children all due to their own limited vision. It's better to expect the best and encourage your co-parent to live up to these expectations. Your children will be the beneficiaries of your good will.

Language

A third obstacle to realignment has to do with the language of divorce. For example, many divorced parents refer to their former spouse as "my ex." By using this term, emphasis continues to be placed on the marital relationship. Its focus is on the relationship that existed in the past. Since there is a continuing relationship between the parents of the child, a better phrase to emphasize the present would be "my child's other parent," or "my child's father (mother)" or "my co-parent."

In the column on the left there are several words or phrases that prevent realignment. For each example listed, change it to a phrase that is more compatible with realignment.

Problem language   **Change to**

1. My ex-(wife, husband)

2. I used to have a family ...

3. They are from a broken home.

4. My children visit me.

5. My children come to see me on ...

6.____ has custody of the children.

7. Failed marriage

8. Visitation agreement/Custody agreement

Another example are the words used to describe the new family arrangement. When one parent says, "My kids don't live with me anymore. Their mother has custody," the speaker sounds like he is no longer an important member of the family. Look how the emphasis changes when a parent instead says, "My kids live with their other parent during the week and with me on the weekend." If you are the parent who sees your children on the weekend, do you think you'd be cooperative with your co-parent if you thought that he/she still has a family and you don't? Wouldn't you be vengeful? Language really makes a difference in attitudes.

After you complete the exercise, circle the problem language that you might use. Now focus on a healthier expression. Remember, your child will also reflect these changes.

Refusal to Realign

The last obstacle to realignment, then, is a parent's refusal to emotionally disengage. This occurs because the parent is getting something out of the continued attachment. He or she obtains a benefit for his or her own purposes. He gets a sense of power when he uses methods of control. It may be a way to get attention when she plays the victim or an attempt to get revenge for being hurt in the past. In children we call these actions misbehavior; in adults we say it's an inappropriate way to meet their needs. Let's see how that works.

Poor Me

Oh, I did everything right. I gave him the best years of my life . . . and what did I get? Kicked in the teeth! Why do these things always happen to me? He wanted the divorce, not me.

She has always used me. She said she loved me but she didn't. She never did . . .

I can't afford to take you to the movies like your father can because he's got all the money.

I just can't do it on my own. I can't raise these kids on the money he gives me. I helped him through school. Now what do I get? Dumped for his secretary. Life isn't fair, even when you do everything right.

Do you see what is similar about these examples? The speakers are playing the part of victim, manipulating others into giving them undue attention. Why? Because they get a payoff for this behavior. They get the reward of attention from family and friends who rush to their aid. In fact, the attention is so rewarding that seeking attention for themselves takes precedence over the needs of their children.

Control

I'll send the child support when I'm good and ready!

I don't have to show you his report card; you can call the teacher.

I know I said you could take the kids on vacation, but I've changed my mind.

I don't have to tell you who her doctor is. It doesn't say anything in the court order.

It says in the court order that you're supposed to call between 7 and 8:00. Its 8:10 so you can't talk to her.

What do these speakers have in common? The sense of being in control of someone else is their pay-off. They enjoy the rush of power they get when they make everyone else bend to their will. They refuse to detach because that would mean giving up the power. Unfortunately, this demand for power increases conflict and it puts the parent's needs before the needs of the children. They get hurt in the crush.

Revenge

Last time you were 20 minutes late, so I'm going to make you wait 20 minutes!

You didn't tell me about Jason's home run, so I'm not going to tell you about his grade in algebra.

When the child's with me I can decide the style of hair cut to get him. I've decided to get him a buzz. (That will really tick her off.)

I've decided to invite Alex (son) to be in the wedding, but I'd rather not have Jennifer (daughter); she's too much like her mother and it just wouldn't work.

What do these speakers have in common? They are all out for revenge. These parents believe that their right to strike back takes precedence over anyone else's rights, even their children's. Getting their revenge is the short-term payoff they receive, even though it may start a revenge cycle that makes things worse.

It's their opportunity to get even and they're taking it, despite the fact that the one who gets hurt the most can be the child in the middle. They refuse to disengage because they would have to give up the right to get even. Instead they stay emotionally engaged for the purpose of satisfying their own needs and consequently hurt the children, whose needs come second.

Do you often take one of these positions? If you are in continuing conflict with your former spouse then one of these patterns may be the one that keeps you engaged. You may need help from a therapist or counselor in order to identify and break your pattern.

Remember you have the power to change. You and your children will be the beneficiaries of your decision.

Taking a Position Rather than an Interest

The last but still important way to determine your level of disengagement and realignment is to imagine yourself in several situations and determine your own potential action. Read the situations below. Determine the action you'd take, then decide if you acted out of your child's best interest or out of your own self-interest. Did you take a position because it satisfied your own need or did you choose an action which clearly was in the best interest of your child? Record your actions below.

Example 1

Your child walks in the door and says, "Daddy's new girlfriend can get free tickets to the circus!"

Step 1. First think about reacting in your own self-interest. What would you say or do? Write down your reactions on page 77 next to "Example 1" in the left column.

For example, you might become bitter and say, "Your father always finds girlfriends who can pay his way." Or, you may find a way to block the visit.

Step 2. Now think about taking an action based on your child's best interests. What would you say or do? Write down your reactions below next to "Example 1" in the right column. For example, you might say, "I'm glad you will be able to see the circus."

Example 2

Your child's band concert is scheduled for an evening that falls during the time he lives with you. Your son asks you if he can invite his mother/father to the concert.

Step 1. Think about reacting in your own self-interest. What would you say or do? Write down your reactions below next to "Example 2" in the left column. For instance, you might become angry and say, "No, it is not your mother's/father's night to see you!" Or, you might play the victim and say, "Well, I guess you can, but you know how nervous I get when your father is around."

Step 2. Now think about taking an action based on your child's best interests. What would you say or do? Write down your reactions below next to "Example 2" in the right column. For instance, you might say, "Sure, it will be nice for your mother/father to see how much you have accomplished this year in band."

SELF INTEREST (Position)	CHILD INTEREST (Interest)
If you took a position of self interest, what would you do?	If you took the position of your child's best interest, what would you do?
Example 1 Say?/Do?	Say?/Do?
Example 2 Say/Do?	Say?/Do?

What to Do to Improve Realignment

To help you base more of your decisions on your child's best interests rather than your own, use the following method. It's called the STP-A technique. It stands for Stop, Think, Pause and Act.

STP-A Technique

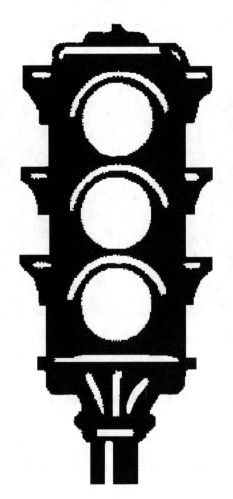

Step 1. STOP

When a situation suddenly occurs, such as your child's other parent calling and saying he/she wants to change the visitation schedule this month, the first thing to do is to STOP yourself from reacting immediately. Try to block out any thoughts and just get yourself to stop temporarily. Take a breath and focus on calming yourself. Try saying to yourself, "Oh, a chance to practice STP-A."

Step 2. THINK

Now is the time to start thinking. Think about the long-term goal for your child. Envision the words "long term" in front of your eyes as you consider the situation. Next think about what you'd do in a business relationship. Picture how you'd act if you were both in business suits in the middle of a group of business people. Now double-check your thinking by then asking yourself, "Am I trying to get something for myself here or can I put my interests aside temporarily to put my child's interests first?"

Step 3. PAUSE

Now take another breath while you pause. Let it out slowly. Keep yourself from reacting. A fast comeback is not useful. Act as if you are almost in slow motion. The pause will seem longer than it really is. Clear your head by exhaling your emotions.

Step 4. ACT

Now you are ready to take action. You may want to ask for time to consider the situation if you are unclear or if you are concerned with your ability to handle your emotions. If in doubt ask for time. Request an appointment to discuss the matter. If you choose to respond, just remember to use non-blaming "I" statements. If you choose to wait, plan to meet in a public place. Consider alternative actions and problem-solving techniques. Then when you've decided what is truly in your child's best interest, take action.

In chapter 3 we looked at the importance of letting go of the old marital relationship. In this chapter we examined the realignment of a new relationship as co-parents. In order to create this realignment as co-parents, you will need to let go and disengage emotionally from the co-parent. It is extremely difficult, and sometimes almost impossible, to use business skills when you are emotionally charged. Use everything you've learned so far in this book and add new tools to your toolbox as you read the remaining chapters in this guide.

 # Exercise

MY BUSINESS-LIKE BEHAVIORS

The six qualities of a business relationship include:

- Dedication to a Common Goal
- Commitment to a Win-Win Relationship
- Negotiation of Differences
- Focus on a Single Topic
- Observation of Common Courtesies
- Communication with Facts, Not Feelings

Directions: Keep track of your interactions with the co-parent. Watch for the six qualities of a business relationship. Focus on what you do to make the interactions more effective. Record your behaviors below. You may include phone contact with your co-parent. At this point do not worry about the outcome of the interactions, just concentrate on learning new skills. Remember, you can only control your behaviors.

Date   **Skill**

CONFUSION OF MIXED MESSAGES

When you are not disengaged, you may communicate mixed messages to your child. The messages below are mixed messages. They are usually spoken in the same day by the same parent.

Directions: Circle the message you think will speak the loudest, (A) or (B). If it is difficult to determine which message your child will hear and remember, put yourself in your child's shoes. Just imagine how anxious and confused you would feel if you were your child.

(A)	(B)
"It's OK to love your dad even though I don't love him."	"I wish he'd fall off the face of the earth!"

(A)	(B)
"It's not your fault that we got a divorce."	"Your mother can't handle you!"

(A)	(B)
"You know you have to go to your dad's house. Don't worry about me. Have lots of fun!"	"I'll really miss you while you are at your dad's. I'll just stay here and wait for you to come home."

(A)	(B)
"These are grown-up matters. Don't worry yourself, your mother and I will take care of things."	"Let me know if your mother has been calling her attorney again, OK?"

(A)	(B)
"Respect your father!"	"He is such a jerk! I'm so glad I'm not married to him anymore!"

(A)	(B)
"I'll always love you."	"You make me so angry when you act just like your MOTHER!"

Remember actions (tone and body language) will <u>always</u> speak louder than words!

CLARIFYING BOUNDARIES

In a business relationship you generally have a sense of boundaries. In the past you and your co-parent shared an intimate relationship. That makes it difficult to establish new boundaries—new rules for the relationship. To realign your relationship as co-parents, boundaries must be addressed. As you realign your relationship it will be difficult to determine what is and is not your business. The following activity may help you and your co-parent clarify your boundaries.

Directions: Read each item below and decide if you should discuss the issue with your co-parent. Assume that you and the co-parent have a joint legal arrangement. Remember you and your co-parent are business partners. It may be difficult to determine if you should or should not address the issue. When in doubt, assume that it is NOT your business. Place an X under the appropriate column.

ISSUE	My Business?	Not My Business?

1. The co-parent got a new job.

2. The co-parent is dating.

3. You are not sure who is sitting for your child when the co-parent is out.

4. You are not sure how the co-parent is spending the child-support money.

5. You wonder how late the co-parent stays out in the evening.

6. The co-parent has been going out drinking when the children are with you.

7. The co-parent took the children boating without life jackets.

8. The co-parent has changed pediatricians.

9. The co-parent is going on a vacation without the children.

10. The co-parent has someone spending the night when the children are in the home.

11. The co-parent has arranged summer camp for the children.

Dear Mom and Dad,

It is good to hear you talk to each other about what is best for me. I hated to hear you yelling at each other all the time. I know you won't always agree about what is best for me, but I can tell that you are keeping your focus on me instead of each other. I feel much better. This is one less thing for me to worry about!

Thanks so much!
Your happy kid,
XXXXXOOOOOXXXXX

Chapter Four Review

1. What does it mean to realign your relationship?

2. What are the six characteristics of a business relationship?

3. Are you willing to treat your co-parent as an equal partner (no matter the custody arrangement) in the business of raising your child/ren?

4. Why are assumptions about divorce so destructive? Which ones do you hold on to?

5. Are you able to recognize when you are acting on revenge, asserting control or playing the victim?

6. How do you know when you are taking a position rather that an interest? How will this impact the co-parenting relationship?

7. What does STP-A stand for?

8. Have you and your co-parent clarified your own expectations regarding appropriate boundaries between the two of you and between the two households?

5.

Neither Fight Nor Take Flight
Managing My Anger

5.

Managing My Own Anger
(Neither Fight nor Take Flight)

Anger. Who hasn't experienced it? Like a storm brewing on the horizon, it makes our adrenaline surge and, at the same time, terrifies us with its potential for destruction. And like that storm, anger seems to appear out of nowhere, bowl us over, then leave again. And while both anger and storms are common experiences for everyone, there is one major difference: anger can be tamed, placed under our control and put to good use.

Activity: *What is Anger?*

Write down everything you know about anger: how you react, what you notice about other people, what triggers anger, etc.

_____

_____

_____

_____

_____

_____

_____

What is this thing called anger? Most people would say that it's an emotion; after all we usually say, "I feel angry." Yet when asked to describe it, people use words and phrases describing what they see: ". . . looked tense, brow furrowed, jaw set, hands clenched, red face, veins bulging, feet planted firmly"; or what others do: "He was so mad he threw a vase at me," "She was kicking and punching," "He slammed the door," "She yelled and screamed," "She threatened me with a knife."

What most people recognize as an emotion on the inside is expressed in words, voice tone and actions on the outside. We all remember what our mother looked like when she was angry, even if no words were spoken. We know what our former spouse sounds like when he/she is angry by the tone of voice used, even when we can't hear which words are being hurled at us. We all know the sting of words spoken or that "cut us to the quick." In studies with adults, it's been shown that the tone of voice carries more of the meaning than even the words chosen.

Activity: *Signs of Anger*

Can you see anger? How can you tell if someone else is angry? Categorize the ways your co-parent expresses anger. What are some signs indicated in his or her body language? What do you notice about her tone of voice? What do you notice about the words he chooses? Write your response below.

1. Body language

_____

_____

_____

2. Tone of Voice

_____

_____

_____

3. Words

_____

_____

_____

Which has the greatest impact?

Try this experiment: Say in a sugary sweet tone, "You're a mean little doggy aren't you?" Now repeat this statement using a firm and angry tone: "You're a sweet, sweet thing." Which example would make your little puppy wag its tail and lick your fingers? I'll wager it's not the second one. Although the words were sweet, I think you'd find the little puppy cowering in the corner. Our children, of course, react the same way. The language spoken by the body and the tone speaks loudest of all.

So is anger an emotion or an action? It's an inner feeling that may get translated into action. It's a force, like a cyclone, starting at a point in the middle, picking up energy until finally it has to let some of that energy go, and it does . . . somewhere, somehow. It may become a constructive force, like the breeze that blows out the fog allowing clear skies to show through, or it may become destructive, like the tornado that destroys everything in its path.

Anger and Divorce

Anger and divorce. Divorce and anger. The two seem to go together like hand and glove or like thunder and lightning. It would be hard to find a divorced man or woman who hasn't experienced the storms of anger. But it might be surprising to learn of the number who are still engulfed in anger storms ten years or more later.

And what kind of anger is it? It's the kind that blinds. It's the kind that hurts, maims and kills. It's the kind that seeps out like toxin from nuclear waste, poisoning everything beneath the surface. It's the kind that destroys everything in its path including the men, women or children who happen to be there. It's the kind that can lead to self-destruction, too.

Why do some people get caught in the middle of the storm while others find a place where the wind dies down? Why do some use their anger to get them moving while others get used by their own anger? Where does this mysterious force come from? And how can the energy from it be harnessed and used productively for the benefit of all?

This chapter will answer these questions and give you the tools to control the force of your own anger. You'll get to decide how to use your anger and decide whether or not to use it constructively to meet your goals. You'll discover techniques that will let you master your anger and be the one in command. Anger will no longer control you; you'll be the one who has the power in your own hands. Using the skills you learn in this chapter and develop further in the following two chapters, you'll be able to protect your children from this deadly force and let it help you move down your path to a better life.

First Signs of Your Own Anger

How can you tell when you're starting to feel angry? What are the first signs that you're starting to experience this emotion called anger? Is it a tightness in your neck, your brow, or your jaw? Is it a feeling of adrenaline that blocks out everything else and gives you a false sense of power? Is it the realization that your foot is tapping on the floor or your fingers are drumming on the table? Is it a sudden blinding of your vision or burst of energy that seems to require that you take some action?

Think of time slowing down and see if you can identify your own signs that anger is on the horizon.

Activity: First Signs of Anger

How can you tell you're starting to feel angry? What are the first signs?

_____

_____

_____

_____

_____

Triggers

Now that you've identified your own first signs, think back. What triggered that outburst of energy? What kicked off the rush of adrenaline? What happened just prior to your teeth grinding or your fists clenching? Whatever happened prior to your anger building was the trigger for your anger. A trigger doesn't necessarily cause the anger, like a burning match doesn't cause a forest fire, but it can be used to start one. See if you can identify hot buttons that are pushed by your former spouse. Write down the ones that set you off.

Then see if you can also identify the triggers for your co-parent. What are his/her hot buttons? What starts his fire or fuels her flames? Write down your guesses in the space below.

Anger Triggers

What are the triggers in your relationship with your co-parent that cause you the most disappointment, frustration, hurt, sadness or fear?

My Triggers

1._____

2 _____

3._____

What do you think are some of your co-parent's triggers that cause him/her the most sadness, hurt, frustration, disappointment or fear?

Co-Parent Triggers

1._____

2 _____

3._____

Anger Progression

What did you discover about your anger triggers, the points in the middle of a cyclone around which energy starts to swirl and build? You may have learned that certain issues are your hot buttons: maybe concern over your child's safety, your own hurt if your former spouse had an affair, a tone of voice that puts you down or shows a lack of respect, a phrase that reminds you of your own insecurities or of disappointment with some of the choices you made. Let's see what happens next in the process as the anger storm builds. Look at the cartoon on the next page.

What would you say is the trigger for the bear in the drawing? What sets him off? It looks like he's trying to get some honey and can't reach it. While that fact is the trigger, he isn't angry immediately, is he? First he experiences another emotion, frustration. It's the frustration that gets his heart pounding and his adrenaline surging. He's frustrated because he wants the honey and he can't get to it. The more frustrated he gets, the more he reacts in a rage, violently shaking the tree and sending the honeycomb right out of the picture.

Frustration was at the core of his anger, and when the frustration wasn't relieved or the problem causing the frustration wasn't resolved, the frustration gathered steam and blew up into an angry reaction.

Can you identify the core emotions at the center of your own flare-ups? Did the trigger touch a sensitive spot of vulnerability? Are you hurt because your former spouse initiated the divorce, embarrassed because he/she left you for a younger woman/man, sad and disappointed that your dream of the perfect family has been destroyed, or scared that you won't be able to survive financially on your own?

Whether or not we're aware of the emotion at the core of our anger, we can be sure that it's there. Left unresolved, it can gather strength and transform itself into rage. Does that mean anger is inevitable? Was it inevitable that the bear's frustration turned to anger? No, there could have been many other conclusions to the cartoon scenario. He might have walked away—and perhaps found some berries to eat nearby or caught a fish in the stream for lunch instead. If he were human, he might have solved the problem in other ways: cultivating beehives in ground-level containers or donning protective garb and climbing a ladder to get to the honeycomb. Either action would have reduced the core frustration and allowed the bear to attain his goal of securing his food.

If that explanation sounds complicated, don't worry. For now, just be aware **that the problem or the trigger** (the honeycomb being out of reach) **doesn't automatically cause the anger.** Instead it triggers an emotion that's central to our core being. Then we either hide behind anger to cover up our hurt, disappointment or frustration. It makes us feel more powerful, even when it doesn't get us what we want. That's sometimes more comfortable than feeling vulnerable at the core. It may not solve the problem, but it keeps us so busy that we no longer feel like we have to solve the problem. Once we allow the anger to brew, it takes on a life of its own. Yet the problem doesn't go away; the bear is still hungry.

Expressions of Anger

As mentioned earlier, anger felt on the inside eventually gets expressed on the outside. All that energy just has to go somewhere, and it does. It often gets expressed verbally, in words and tone of voice, and in actions. It may be directed with full force toward someone else or it may be directed toward oneself. It can be diverted or deflected or even used to pull someone else into its black hole.

Sarcasm is one expression of anger; rolling one's eyes, shrugging one's shoulders and emitting a huge sigh are other, more subtle expressions. More overt actions include shoving, punching, or holding someone in a position that prevents free movement. Slamming doors and manipulating situations can express anger. Below are seven common expressions of anger.

After reading their descriptions, decide which description best illustrates the pattern that you usually use to express your anger and note it on the bottom of the page. For now it's helpful to identify the style of expression that you use. Later we'll look back at this page for greater understanding.

Expressions of Anger

The following are different ways that people use their anger. As you read these styles, focus on your personal style rather than your co-parent's.

1. HOLD IT

People who hold onto their anger are those who wish to avoid conflict. They try to avoid looking at the underlying or core problem and refuse to address it or solve it. They often become depressed or ill with headaches, stomachaches or other physical symptoms. Young people whose parents who hold their anger don't learn that there are ways to solve problems. Instead their role models demonstrate holding onto the tension, not daring to face it and deal with it.

_____

_____

_____

2. EXPLODE IT

People who explode their anger express it through abusive means. They scream, throw things, push, shove, kick and hit other people, sometimes even choke, slap or threaten to kill. Sometimes they commit murder. Other exploders are violent with words. They leave emotional scars that last a lifetime. Exploders are unpredictable, flaring up with little notice or at unpredictable times. The violence may be directed at the co-parent or may even be directed at the child or teenager in the family. Family members of the exploder are generally anxious and vigilant, ever watchful for the next attack. These children are constantly fearful that they or someone close to them may get hurt. If they try to rescue the victim, they can be hurt as well.

Exploders Continuum

Yell - Verbal Abuse - Threaten - Throw Things - Push - Corner - Slap - Hit - Punch - Beat - Homicide

←———————————————————————————————————→

3. DUMP IT THERE

 People who dump their anger on others usually use blame as their dump truck. They put down the efforts of others or the inherent value of others. They find someone to blame for any of their problems; the someone could be the co-parent, the in-laws, their own parents, the system, the teachers, the school or whoever is in the line of fire. They attempt to induce guilt so they themselves do not have to take responsibility for the situation. Children of parents who dump their anger often have low self-esteem because they believe they are at fault whenever there is a problem.

4. DUMP IT HERE

 Other parents dump their anger on themselves. Possibly they were children of the parents described above and believe that any problem is of their own making. They soak up the problems but they don't try to solve them. They just gather them and become victims. *It's all my fault, I should have . . ., I could have . . .* are their favorite sentences. *I'm so stupid . . ., Look what I've done . . .* are other common phrases in their speech. They seem more obsessed with assuming the guilt than with doing anything to relieve the problem.

5. DIVERT IT

 Parents who divert anger find a way to express it in manipulative and devious ways. They pull a third person into the triangle, trying to get someone else angry. They won't deal directly with anger, instead preferring to have someone else carry it out overtly. They try to get their children or their parents or their friends angry at their former spouse rather than show their anger directly. In these families there is also a lot of tension, with the people involved feeling like they've done something wrong, but they can't quite figure out what it is. Kids can also be diverters, drawing in one parent who then becomes angry at the other.

6. DENY IT

Deniers are good at masking their anger. They try to convince themselves as well as everyone else that their anger doesn't exist. As a matter of fact, they are so reluctant to allow themselves to be uncomfortable that they try to cut off any emotion rather than put themselves in a position where the core emotion makes them feel vulnerable. Fear, hurt or frustration are not part of their vocabulary or of their existence. They appear tough or unfeeling and almost never talk about emotions or feelings. Often they use drugs or alcohol to numb their feelings. Children of deniers learn to get on with their lives, but at the consequence of becoming robot-like and denying the emotional flavor of human existence.

7. SOLVE IT

Problem-solvers can admit that they are angry and can try to identify the core emotion that developed into anger. They can look beneath the surface to the root cause and identify the real problem that needs to be solved. They do not deny the full range of negative emotions like hurt, sadness, disappointment or frustration, but after acknowledging their own feeling, they start thinking about actions which can lead to a solution to the problem. They use their anger constructively to give them energy to solve the problem. When they do feel angry, they find appropriate means to let it go. Children who live with parents who are solvers learn that there are ways to use their anger to work for them.

What are the one or the two ways that describe how you express anger?

_____

_____

Anger: Helpful or Hurtful

Constructive Uses of Anger

It is often said that people don't have anger; instead, they use their anger. Anger can be used either constructively or destructively. Do you ever think of using your anger constructively?

As we said, anger provides a surge of adrenaline; it gets us revved up and ready to act. That can be valuable. Someone in a depressed state following divorce could use some of that anger to get moving again, to propel herself toward taking some action. Action means making something change, and we all resist change. When faced with the need for change, people are like immovable objects: they require a force to get the inert mass to overcome the resistance. Anger provides that force.

Anger can provide the motivation (or motive-for-action) for getting a better job, seeking companionship with friends, asking someone for a date. It can overcome reluctance to assert oneself, to set limits or boundaries, to ask for what one wants. It can force people to push through their fears, make decisions, reach their goals. Anger can help a person overcome obstacles and do the things that will solve the initial problem. A woman, afraid to demonstrate her ambition, is propelled to reach for greater achievements following comments by her former spouse that hint at her lack of competence. A man, unsure of his parenting skills, is so angered by his former wife's jabbing at his vulnerability that he enrolls in a parenting education class and becomes more of an expert than she.

In each of these examples, the power of anger was used constructively to solve the initial problem. With the initial problem solved, the accompanying emotion (hurt, disappointment, fear) subsided and anger no longer appeared on the horizon.

Constructive Uses Of Anger Activity

Describe one time that your anger helped you take a positive action:

_____

_____

_____

Destructive Uses of Anger

Although anger can be used constructively, it can also be used destructively. Look at the cartoon below.

Example A

The prairie dog's core or primary emotion: _____

The prairie dog's action: _____

When the prairie dog was first threatened, he probably felt annoyed. His feelings turned into assertion, with the prairie dog taking a stance warning the predator to keep its distance. The predator, in turn, decided to back down and move away. Now look at the next cartoon.

Example B

The prairie dog's core or primary emotion _____

The prairie dog's action: _____

The result _____

Which situation did the prairie dog deal with his anger constructively? ___A or ___B

What was the result?_____

Rather than take a stance and set his own boundaries this time, what did the prairie dog do instead? He allowed his emotional response to turn to rage, attacking his foe. The result was a bloody one with life hanging in the balance.

When the prairie dog used his anger to set his boundaries assertively, he acted in a constructive manner. But when he used his anger to fuel his attack, the consequences were destructive for both animals. Just think what would have happened if the prairie dog had young pups; he might not be able to care for and protect them. Anger in humans can have the same destructive results.

Methods of Destruction

Anger has many methods of destruction. One is to hurt someone directly, either through a physical assault or through an emotional attack on someone's self-esteem. For example, saying "You never were a good provider" to a former spouse.

Another is to begin a revenge cycle; for example, one parent brings a suit to obtain more child support; the other retaliates by bringing a suit against the co-parent for gaining custody. The cycle continues to escalate.

A third destructive use of anger is to turn the anger inward and go into a depression, thereby proving that the former spouse caused the problem.

Read back over the seven expressions of anger on the previous pages and on the lines below each one write down how that anger expression can be destructive to: 1) oneself, 2) one's child and 3) someone else. Take note of your own methods of expression and the results they bring. (If you allow yourself to focus on your co-parent's anger, it will increase your own anger with potentially destructive results for yourself! Remember the prairie dog.)

Anger in Divorce

Example 1:

A woman had been married for 24 years and had never worked outside the home. Her husband initiated the divorce. She is very unsettled about the insecurity of providing a living for herself. Often she is very angry at her co-parent, blaming him for her present situation.

- What is the woman's inner or primary emotion?
- What action could she take which would start to relieve her inner emotion?
- If she gets into an angry state, what are some things she might say and do?
- Which action is constructive?
- Which action is destructive?

Example 2:

A man found his wife in bed with another man. He has always been faithful and is extremely hurt. When he thinks about his marriage he gets very angry.

- What is the man's inner emotion?
- What are some actions he could take to relieve his inner emotion?
- When he gets into an angry state about his marriage, what are some things he might say or do?
- Which action is constructive?
- Which action is destructive?

Example 3.

A woman found out from her children after their last visit that her former spouse has remarried a much younger woman. They have only been divorced one month. She is sure that she will never remarry. When she gets upset over her situation, she goes round and round about the unfairness of life.

- What is the woman's inner emotion?
- What action could she take to start relieving her inner emotion?
- If she gets into an angry state, what are some things she might say and do?
- Which action is constructive?
- Which action is destructive?

Staying Stuck in Anger

In the last chapter we mentioned that anger is one of the stages of grief. What would happen to a person if he or she got stuck in that stage and couldn't move on? He wouldn't be able to improve his situation or increase his own happiness; she wouldn't be able to solve old problems and gain the accompanying benefits as a result.

What about the children? How much does the fear of upsetting their parents or the dread of observing another round of parental revenge affect their well-being? Please ask yourself these questions: "Am I stuck in anger? Am I ready to move on?"

Reasons People Don't Move On

It's not an easy task. After all, anger is familiar. It becomes a habit and we all know that habits are hard to break. It's scary to do something different and takes effort to change.

Sometimes a person just doesn't know how to do anything different. He's never had a role model for handling anger any other way; she doesn't know what else to try. Yet the biggest reasons for staying stuck in anger are the following two:

- You have to face the real problem at the core
- You have no one else to blame

To give up anger, a person has to take responsibility. The person has to rely on herself and say, "If it's to be, it's up to me. Even if I got a lousy deal after 20 years of marriage, the rest of my life is what I make it. The past is past; the present is now and I make my future. Although I'm alone, I don't have to be lonely. I may not be financially secure right now, but the effort I make today will determine where I am tomorrow. My children will learn more from a good role model and I choose to be one."

Anger is a Choice

Try doing the next exercise. Write down two sentences that you often say about your relationship with your co-parent starting with the words "I can't," such as "I can't seem to talk civilly with my former spouse."

I can't . . . .

I can't . . . .

Now go back and repeat the same sentences, saying them aloud and **substituting the word "won't"** for the word "can't." How did you react? Many people choke over the words when they realize that it really is a decision they can make. Some even fight the idea. Then, after a pause, the result is often one of complete and total freedom. If the choice is mine, I am free to choose the result I want. I no longer am controlled by anyone else. I no longer choose to be caught in an anger trap or a revenge cycle. I can choose another direction and I do.

If you followed this line of thinking, you may also be terrified right now. While you had a comfortable pattern of acting, knowing what to expect and who to blame, you now have a vacuum where that pattern once was. The rest of this chapter will be devoted to filling that vacuum with techniques and tools designed to replace the ones you left behind.

You may find that your entire future takes on a brighter look wherever you turn. Soon you will realize that you are in control; no one else can make you angry anymore. You will still feel the richness of emotions, positive and negative, but you no longer will have to turn to anger to protect yourself. You will have more elegant choices of how to react. How to do just that is the topic of the rest of this chapter.

What You Can Do To Manage Your Anger

How does the core emotion turn into anger for some people and not the others? What's the secret?

Imagine that you are sitting in a car in the middle of a traffic jam. Traffic has come to a stop on all sides. You look to the car on your left and see a guy sitting there, bopping to the music. You look at the car ahead of you and you see a woman talking on her car phone. You look at the right and you see a red-faced person scowling, hitting the steering wheel repeatedly and cursing loudly.

The trigger—the traffic jam—is the same for everybody. Yet there are three different feelings evident: pleasure (Music Man), energized (Phone Woman) and anger (Red-faced Person). The diagram below shows these different responses. Which block is still missing?

TRIGGER	BELIEFS	FEELINGS	ACTIONS
A. Traffic jam		Pleasure	Bopping to the music
B. Traffic jam		Energized	Talking on car phone
C. Traffic jam		Angry	Hitting & cursing

The trigger, such as the traffic jam, doesn't cause the emotion, since the people involved all experienced different emotions. Albert Ellis, the founder of rational-emotive therapy, introduced a simple model to help people take responsibility for their reactions by restructuring their beliefs. Basically, Ellis stated that the trigger such as the traffic jam, does not cause the emotion, since the people involved all experienced different emotions.

Possible Thoughts or Beliefs:

    A. Probably believed that traffic jams gave him a chance to enjoy listening to his music

    B. Probably thought that she was smart to get a car phone so that she could make use of these precious minutes

    C. Probably believed that traffic jams shouldn't happen, that someone ought to do a better job planning traffic flow (blaming), and that some jerk probably did something stupid to cause an accident. What is the result of his own beliefs? He gets increasingly frustrated and upset and misses out on all the benefits (pleasure or work accomplished) he could obtain by thinking other thoughts.

Beliefs and Thoughts

Most people aren't even aware that these thoughts are swirling around in their heads. They think that the trigger automatically makes them feel a certain way. However, it is your beliefs or your thoughts about an event or situation that make you act a certain way. Let's say it's snowing outside right now. What could you be thinking? You might be nervous because you don't want to drive in it to get home tonight. You might be excited because you could go skiing tomorrow. You might feel peaceful thinking about sitting in front of the fire you'll build at home this evening.

Yet if a person started screaming and yelling because he or she believed that the snow would cover the world and everyone would be smothered to death, you would probably say that those beliefs weren't accurate. They were distorted beliefs.

TRIGGER	BELIEFS	FEELINGS	ACTIONS
A. Snowfall		nervous	go home ASAP
B. Snowfall		excited	go skiing
C. Snowfall		peaceful	build a fire
D. Snowfall		devastated	scream/yell

Again, the trigger (snowfall) doesn't cause the emotion, since the people involved all experienced different emotions. What caused the emotions is the thoughts that occurred between the trigger and the feelings. Fill in the blank spaces guessing what thoughts or beliefs caused the emotions.

Possible Thoughts or Beliefs:

A. The snowfall would create dangerous road conditions

B. The snowfall created the opportunity for skiing

C. The snowfall offered the chance to go home, build a fire and curl up in front of the fire with a good book

D. The snow would cover the world and everyone would smother to death.
   (This is an example of a "distorted belief." It distorts the real situation.)

Distorted Beliefs

Let's look at another situation. A father brings his son back to the mother's house after the child has spent the weekend with him. The child starts crying uncontrollably when the father leaves. What is one thought the mother could have? Write your answer down under the space provided in the Recognizing Beliefs Activity below.

She might think that the father had said negative things about her and turned the child against her. As a result she would likely feel upset and angry at the father and might act negatively toward him. Is this accurate or distorted? We don't know, but we do know the result of the beliefs.

What might be another thought someone else could have? Another person might have believed that the child has difficulty making the transition and seeing any parent leave. As a result she would be feeling compassionate toward the child and would probably try to comfort him.

Recognizing Beliefs Activity

Example 1: Young son starts crying when father drops him off at his mother's home.

Mother:

TRIGGER	BELIEFS	FEELINGS	ACTIONS
1. Son crying	"He made our son cry again!"	anger	yells at father
2. Son crying	"Our son doesn't want to leave his father."	sadness	comforts son
3. Son crying			
4. Son crying			

Example 2: A couple has been divorced about a year. The father and daughter are at a restaurant and they run into mother with a man.

Father:

TRIGGER	BELIEFS	FEELINGS	ACTIONS
1. Mother with man	"She is a real tramp!"	rage	accuses mother
2. Mother...	"She is making friends."	relief	friendly smile
3. Mother...			
4. Mother...			

Changing Distorted Beliefs Activity

An event, situation or a person cannot cause you to feel nervous, angry, depressed or devastated. Your thoughts determine your feelings and actions. And that is the good news. Since our beliefs cause our emotions, which lead to actions, we can choose to change our actions by changing our beliefs. So, a change in beliefs causes a change in actions.

It's especially important, when anger occurs, to examine the beliefs that lead to that feeling. The next step is to determine if your belief is distorted. One way to tell if your belief is unrealistic is by listening for a few key words in those beliefs. They include words like "ought," "should," "never," and "always." Challenging our distorted or unrealistic beliefs and replacing them with thoughts that are more realistic is one of the ways to manage anger and distress.

Change each of the following distorted belief statements to one that is more realistic. Some have been done for you.

Distorted Belief	Realistic Belief
He ought to give me more money than he does. →	He gives me what the courts decided. I might think it's unfair but that only makes me upset; it doesn't change anything. If I need more money, I'll have to find a way to earn it.
She ought to let our son spend more time with me. →	
He ought to care more about things like rules and bedtime and such. →	
She ought to be more flexible. →	
He should do more for us. →	Even if I think he could do more for us, we will learn how to make it on our own.
He shouldn't go fishing on his days with the kids. →	
She shouldn't go off with her friends when she's got the kids. →	
I'll never get over him. →	Even though it feels like it will be difficult, I can learn to be independent.
I'll always be poor. →	I may not have much money right now but…
She'll never be a caring mother →	

Changing distorted beliefs to constructive thoughts is very difficult. It is hard to break old patterns. Sometimes our distorted beliefs bring us comfort because we don't have to take responsibility for our actions. We may fall back into a "victim" role or quickly blame another person instead of accepting that we are the source of our own anger. Overcoming and managing anger by changing your thoughts takes patience and practice. But, most of all, it takes a "leap of faith" and a willingness to give your co-parent the benefit of the doubt. After all, you have everything to gain and nothing to lose but your own personal distress.

Escalating Triggers

For every action there is a reaction. An action becomes another person's trigger. As noted below, the father's action becomes the mother's trigger. Then, the mother's action becomes the father's trigger. The parents' actions become the child's trigger. As the illustration below demonstrates, it is easy to create a situation that quickly escalates to the point of no return. In this situation, the parents are not challenging their beliefs or staying focused on their child. Consequently, the child is pulled into the conflict and, as a result, strengthens his negative beliefs about his parents. Consider the following escalating scene.

Escalating Triggers

	TRIGGER	BELIEF	FEELING	ACTION
Dad:	Son informs him about the missed soccer game	"She wants me to miss his games." "She <u>should</u> try to encourage our relationship	Anger Frustration Disappointment	Calls Mom to accuse her
Mom:	Dad calls in angry accusing manner	"He is such a jerk!" "He <u>never</u> listens!"	Fury Surprise Frustration	Gets defensive, Hangs up
Dad:	Mom hangs up on Dad	'She is up to her usual games." "I will <u>never</u> trust her!"	Fury	Curses, Complains out loud about Mom
Child:	Hears Dad yell saying bad things about Mom	"My Dad isn't interested in me or my game." "They will <u>always</u> hate each other."	Hurt Sad Anger Frustration	Throws soccer ball and leaves the room
Dad:				

Challenge: Now, take the child's action and let it trigger Dad.

Challenging Beliefs

The situation can be turned around by the parents' willingness to challenge their internal beliefs. To do this, one or both parents must take a "leap of faith," avoid assumptions, consider alternatives and focus on their child. Take a second look. Which scene do you want to be part of?

	TRIGGER	BELIEF	FEELING	ACTION
Dad:	Son informs him about the missed soccer game	"My son is disappointed that I missed his game." I need to find out why I wasn't told."	Disappointment Irritation	Listens to son, Calls Mom next day
Mom:	Dad calls using a neutral tone of voice	"He really wanted to be at our son's game." "He wants an explanation."	Regret Shame	Calmly answers Dad's questions
Dad:	Mother calmly answers Dad's questions	"She is willing to work with me."	Satisfaction Hope	Calmly listens to mom
Child:				

Challenge: Now, take the father's first action and let it trigger the son.

Additional Anger Management Strategies

What are some of the other techniques that you personally use to reduce your anger? In the same way that changing your distorted beliefs changes your feelings which influences the actions you take (positive or negative), you can also directly change some actions you take which will influence your thoughts and feelings.

DO

These are some techniques that people often find helpful to break the anger cycle.

1. Breathe deeply and release.

2. Practice STP-A.

3. Write in a journal when you feel angry and need a release.

4. Do something active to channel your anger such as walking, exercising, gardening, cleaning, waxing the car, painting, etc.

5. Find an old telephone book and tear up the pages or break something that is insignificant.

6. Enjoy an anger fantasy.

7. Find someone (other than your child) to talk to when you need support, i.e. friends, family, therapist.

8. Join a support group.

9. Create a ritual to let go of your pain, like burning old photos, releasing a balloon filled with angry thoughts or even with small pieces of paper on which you've written memories which cause you anger. Then decide to "let it go."

10. Find a place where you are alone, such as when you are in your car sitting at a light, and scream. Try different loud sounds until you find one that gives you relief.

11. Try having a good cry, preferably when your child is not home. A massage following the cleansing cry is very helpful.

12. Allow yourself a period of time to feel like a victim, such as one or two days. Be careful not to get stuck in this state longer than the time you've selected.

13. Swear out loud (when you're alone). See if this gives you relief from your anger or makes it worse.

14. Draw mustaches on old photos of the person with whom you are angry. Make lots of copies of an old photo (perhaps your wedding photo) and enjoy thinking of all the things you could do with it. Be creative! Remember, do not let your child know about your ideas or let them find the results of your expression. Do not tell your child's other parent what you are doing. This is only for you.

15. Read books which help you manage and release your anger. You will find a list of resource books in the back of this guide.

16. Write a letter to the person with whom you are angry, stamp the envelope and mail it to some strange address. Have fun with it, such as "Jerk City, USA," or "Divorce Do-Do, USA." Place this hostile letter in the mailbox and say good bye to all your anger. When any angry feelings try to come back visualize dropping another letter in the mailbox.

17. If all else fails, find a large rock, let it represent your angry feelings and place it in your purse or pocket. Do not go anywhere without it. Put it next to your bedside table at night and take it with you to business meetings during the day. No one needs to know about this. Carry it with you for weeks or longer until you get really tired of carrying it. When you are serious about getting rid of your anger, bury the rock in your back yard or throw it in the river.

WARNING: Do not let your child see these behaviors. They are intended to help you with your anger. Do not bring your child into your anger; it will only confuse or frighten your child.

DON'T

1. Do not try to ignore your anger, save your anger, swallow your anger or sweep it under the rug. Do find a way to express your anger and your pain.

2. Do not take your anger out on the wrong person, for example, your child. If you do, forgive yourself, apologize, and make amends.

3. Do not eat, drink or use other substances to numb the pain of anger.

4. Do not discuss your co-parent in a negative or angry manner when your children are present. Do not be fooled into thinking that your children will not hear or understand you; they will.

5. Do not use your children to get even with your co-parent.

6. Do not use your anger to justify sharing negative information about your co-parent with your child. There is **no good reason** for doing this. It will ultimately backfire on you. Let your child discover who his other parent is, in his own time and in his own way.

Remember, anger, like emotional pain, can be useful. We can choose to use it as motivation to do things that will help us get better, or we can choose to hold onto it and keep ourselves bitter. It is up to each one of us to decide.

Anger and Children

Managing Your Anger at Home

It is common for parents to feel confused about managing their own anger when they are around their children. On the one hand, we're told not to deny our feelings, but on the other hand, we know that our anger can upset them or have other negative consequences. Owning your feelings and choosing how to express them are two separate steps. Let's see how that works.

If your child notices that you seem quiet since you got home from work and he asks if you're upset, you can respond in one of several ways. Your tone of voice and body language will give your child the message about the level of your anger. Then the words you choose will add to that message. "Yes, I am upset. I am annoyed with my boss for not letting me take tomorrow off." In this way, you have identified the feeling "annoyance" and the trigger for that feeling. It is useful to your child's development to hear many "feelings" words other than "angry" or "mad." Try to express the core emotion, such as frustrated, worried, annoyed, disappointed and sad. That will help your child better understand his or her own emotions. Then, if your child seems anxious about your feelings, you can reassure her, "There is nothing to worry about. I'll feel better later; right now I just need to be angry (or quiet.)"

It is also important not to share too much information with your child. Children should be protected from receiving information that will cause them distress. For example:

"I've lost my job. I don't know how we're going to make it," would cause your child to feel highly anxious.

"You are making my life miserable," could cause your child to feel responsible for your problems and to feel rejected.

"I really hate your mother!" or "I don't know why I ever married your father!" could cause anxiety, fear and a problem with divided loyalties.

"Sometimes I feel so angry I could kill your father!" or "Your mother has taken everything," can cause significant fear and anxiety.

"You make me so angry when you act like your mother," or "I have to give all my money to your mother for child support," or "Your father never wanted you to be born," would all cause tremendous guilt.

These are impulsive and highly inappropriate expressions of anger to share with your child. The rule of thumb is: **Do not share your anger regarding someone your child loves.** Your child should not become your sounding board or your support system. If that happens, it can be extremely detrimental to the well-being of your child.

Helping Children Manage Their Own Anger

It is also important to help your children learn how to handle their own anger. One of the most important influences on your child's anger management is the way that you *model handling your own anger*. By following the guidelines in this chapter, you'll find that you are becoming an excellent role model for careful management of anger.

A second influence is the protection you provide in *not letting your own anger overwhelm your children* or cause them intense anxiety. By choosing to set limits on your own words and body language, you'll better protect your child from undue stress.

A third influence on your child's ability to manage anger is *the way you respond when your child is angry*. Here is where you can help your child find appropriate expressions for his own anger. First, you need to help your children become aware of their own feelings and be able to identify them. When your child has his or her fists clenched, you can say, "You're really angry that I won't let you go out now." Or, "I can see that you're frustrated in not being able to do what you want when you want."

When your child says, "I hate you!" or 'I hate _____(my other parent)," realize that he is just attempting to express his anger. You can help by not becoming angry yourself. Instead, reframe the hate, changing it to anger. For example, "I can see how angry you are with me for not letting you stay up late. You can be angry but you still need to go to bed." Or "You really are angry with your mother right now. How could you tell her how you feel?"

Some parents *help their young children find appropriate physical expressions*, such as a stuffed animal to hit rather than a person ("People aren't for hitting; you can punch Old Sarge instead, if you want"). Find several expressions that you will allow and suggest them to the child. You can even put pictures up on a poster of things that are OK and things that are not OK to do with anger. Point to the pictures when your child is angry or ask if she wants to draw an angry picture or take apart a take-apart doll.

It's also important to let your children know that they have *permission to express feelings that are different from your own*. When you are angry, it doesn't mean that your child needs to feel angry. Likewise, the opposite is true; when your child feels love for the other parent, you do not need to feel the same. For example, "It's OK for you to love your father even if I do not want to be married to him."

Remember that *anger and discipline do not go together*. When you try to discipline when you are angry, the child might get the message that he/she was powerful enough to make you mad. If that happens, the child has already gotten his reward. It's better to make decisions about discipline when you are not angry so that you can think and communicate clearly about the misbehavior. Then you can let the child know that you were worried that another child might get hurt or concerned that she might get hurt. Then you can set a consequence that's fitting the behavior: "You can come inside to calm down before continuing to play with the neighbors." Or "You can play in the back yard or you can play inside the house (rather than be close to the road)."

SUMMARY

When you manage your own anger in ways that your children can model and when you help your children find ways to identify and express their own feelings of anger, you are equipping them with important life skills. They will be prepared to understand the feelings that cause them the most distress and find expressions of those feelings in ways that safely allow them relief from that distress. Your role as model and teacher will greatly aid them in moving through the experience of divorce and move on with their own lives.

UNDERSTANDING YOUR EMOTIONS

Directions: Read each example carefully. Then mark the response that is most like yours.

A: Trigger   B: Beliefs & Thoughts   C: Emotional Consequences   D: Decisions or Actions

Example #1.

A: While on the phone your co-parent says, "Have you sent the child support check yet? I'm really short this month."

B: You believe that she is simply asking a question, and you resist reading into the comment.

C: You do not feel threatened.

D: You answer directly without emotion.

Or:

A: Same trigger

B: You do not trust the co-parent. You believe he is setting you up to return to court for an increase in support. You believe you are being manipulated.

C: You feel angry or anxious.

D: You snap back at the co-parent and initiate an argument about something else.

Or:

A: Same trigger

B: You believe that you got a rotten deal in the divorce and the co-parent just doesn't realize or appreciate how well she did in the settlement.

C: You feel furious because this question has opened up an old wound.

D: You blame the co-parent and tell her to "drop dead!" You slam down the phone.

UNDERSTANDING YOUR EMOTIONS

Example # 2.

A: You are on the phone with your child when the co-parent says it is time to get off.

B: You believe that the co-parent has been attempting to alienate you from your child. You believe that you and your child will never be close as long as the other parent is in the picture. You know how it feels to lose a parent. You believe that the co-parent will continue to control you and your child forever.

C: You feel angry and discouraged.

D: You call the co-parent on the phone and accuse her of making up excuses to get your child off the phone. You may even threaten to go back to court for custody.

Or:

A: Same trigger

B: You think that your child wanted to get off the phone but waited for the co-parent to request it. You wonder if your child loves the co-parent more than they love you. You also think that the co-parent will always be closer because your child lives with her more than with you. You believe you will never win.

C: You feel hurt, resigned, angry, resentful or depressed.

D: You may respond by rejecting or by spoiling your child during the next visit. You may also become depressed or irritable. You may try to put the co-parent down; this hurts your child.

Or:

A: Same trigger

B: You believe that the request was based on unfinished homework or some other issue. You believe that you and your child will talk tomorrow. You also believe that the co-parent is attempting to value your relationship with your child rather than block it.

C: You feel disappointed and understanding.

D: You ask the co-parent, in a reasonable tone, to let you know when is the best time to call in the evening. You negotiate with the co-parent or you plan to have your child call you instead.

LET'S PRACTICE

Directions: Read each trigger below and the complete the beliefs, emotions and potential actions you might have. Be honest.

Situation #1

A: You ask the co-parent if you can change the date of your next visit because your parents will be in town. You want your child to visit with her grandparents. The co-parent responds by saying only, "No, it is not convenient."

B: Belief

C: Emotions

D: Action

Situation #2

A: You show up for a scheduled meeting with your child's teacher and your co-parent forgets to attend. This type of thing has happened before.

B: Belief

C: Emotions

D: Action

LET'S PRACTICE (*continuation*)

Situation #3

A: Your child refers to her new stepparent as daddy/or mommy.

B: Belief

C: Emotions

D: Action

Situation #4

A: You were the one to file for divorce. Your child asks, "Why don't you love Daddy anymore? He still loves you. Can't we still be a family? Please?"

B: Belief

C: Emotions

D: Action

IDENTIFYING MY CURRENT TRIGGERS

Directions: Identify anger triggers and the thoughts you think immediately before you experience anger, hurt, disappointment, etc. Try to complete at least half of the examples as they pertain to your divorce or parental relationship. You may notice that these triggers may be similar to your "hot buttons."

Current Activating Triggers	Current Beliefs/Thoughts	Current Emotions
1. Parent does not return child's clothes.	He/She will never be responsible. He/She wants to inconvenience me.	Anger, frustration
2.		
3.		
4.		
5.		
6.		
7.		
8.		
9.		
10.		

LEARNING NEW REACTIONS

Directions: Look back at page 110. Place the original activating trigger in the far left column under (A). Now create a new and improved belief regarding the trigger. Force yourself to open up to new possibilities. Do this for your child, not for your co-parent. After you complete each new belief in the middle column, go through each one and label the new emotion you might have if you could use this new belief. This is a very difficult yet important task. Your growth will be influenced by this activity more than any other. An example has been provided.

Original Trigger (A)	New Belief (B)	New Emotion (C)
1. Parent does not return child's clothes.	He/She is washing the clothes. He/She was in a hurry and forgot the clothes.	Partial Understanding Slight Annoyance.
2.		
3.		
4.		
5.		
6.		
7.		
8.		
9.		

TAKING CONTROL OF MY ANGER

Directions: Record the times you took control of your anger. Identify the trigger, beliefs, feelings and actions.

TRIGGER	BELIEFS	FEELINGS	ACTION

TAKING CONTROL OF MY ANGER *(continuation)*

TRIGGER	BELIEFS	FEELINGS	ACTION

Dear Dad and Mom,

Wow, I like what you are doing. If feels really cool when you assume good things about my other parent. It seems like you aren't so mad. I know that sometimes you are sad and worried, but I know that we'll be all right. Thanks for helping me out when I am angry too. It even feels as if you like me more when you say nice things about my other parent. I can breathe a sigh of relief knowing that you can begin to change your thoughts. I appreciate this more than I can ever say. I like knowing that you really care.

Your relieved child

XXXXXOOOOOXXXXX

Chapter Five Review

1. What are your anger triggers? Do you expect your co-parent to avoid your triggers or are you ready to change your reactions? If so, what will you do differently?

2. How do you express your anger and how will this impact your child?

3. What are the negative beliefs you hold to about your co-parent? Are there any themes to the beliefs? Are you ready to loosen your grip on these beliefs? If so, start by changing words like "always" to "sometimes."

4. What actually "causes" your emotional reactions when dealing with your co-parent?

5. Do you recognize that when you say "I can't" you are usually saying "I won't?"

6. Are you effectively managing your anger and your impulses? If not, which of the suggestions in your guide are you willing to try?

7. Do you understand the concept of escalating triggers between you and your co-parent? Do you also understand how your child can become triggered by your behaviors?

6.

Defuse or Light the Fuse
Taking Control of Conflict

6.

Taking Control of Conflict
(Defuse or Light the Fuse)

How Conflict Happens

How do arguments happen? What provides the spark that gets the argument started? And what fuels the fury that keeps it going? If you were asked to design an argument, what would you say happens first? And second? And third?

Some say the tone of voice, a look, or just the right word is all that's needed to start an argument. "His voice, dripping in sarcasm, just set me off," is the way one woman described it. "When she says I'm weak, I go berserk," is another person's description. "The way he jabs his finger in my face, I feel threatened and ready to run to my lawyer for protection," is the description provided by a third. These three: tone of voice, body language or words themselves, are like the matches that light a fire. That little spark that seemed so unimportant at the time gives off just enough heat to get the fire burning.

Now, more fuel is needed to build the fire bigger. The co-parent, slightly singed from the lighted match, quickly fuels the fire with his defensiveness or her counterattack. "I am not weak," is all that's needed to show his hot button has been successfully ignited and he's caught in the fire. "Maybe I am what you say, but you're worse," is another reply that adds fuel to the fire. Now attack and counterattack blow oxygen on the flame and keep it building. The bigger the fire, the harder it becomes to extinguish. That's the same with conflict: the more furious the arguments, the more difficult they are to stop and the more destruction they cause.

"From one little spark a forest fire grows," is the refrain often heard in elementary school fire-prevention classes. The same principle holds true for conflict. A spark that's intended to hurt just a little can light the fuse to a huge explosion.

But a spark without fuel quickly burns itself out. So too the demands of conflict. If the co-parent doesn't add fuel to the fire, the initial spark from the critical comment or the sarcastic tone of voice quickly extinguishes itself and no argument develops. Without defensiveness or attack in a co-parent's response, no fire will burn and the tiny flame will go out. So who's to blame for conflict? Both co-parents provide something to make the fire burn—and both can extinguish the flame.

A comment or action provides the spark; a response provides the fuel. What's the result? The greater the size of the argument, like the larger the fire, the greater the destruction it causes.

Though it may have seemed right to fight fire with fire, both parents can get burned. Both become upset from engaging in conflict; both can get hurt from vengeful comments that result and both can be scarred from the legal battles that often follow.

The victim who gets hurt the most is the child caught in the middle. The child doesn't light the match nor does she fuel the fire. Yet she's the innocent victim who's asleep upstairs while the building burns around her. He feels the heat from the argument but he's powerless to control its destructiveness and helpless to extinguish the fire. She's caught in the middle with all exits blocked.

How can the result be different? Taking a clue from our safety classes, we know of several ways to prevent fires:

- Deciding where and when to communicate and what topics are off-limits can prevent many conflicts from starting.
- "Don't play with matches" is a reminder to eliminate the voice tones, body language or specific words that push your co-parent's hot buttons. Discovering your own hot buttons can help you become vigilant when you are feeling the heat.
- And finally, the phrase "Don't add fuel to the fire" will be our model for responding to initial sparks in ways that extinguish the argument altogether. Listening and reflecting can defuse the conflict and "I" Statements can smother the flame.

Either co-parent can prevent an argument; either one can put the fire out. In this chapter you'll learn techniques for prevention and for extinguishing the fire. Destruction caused by the conflict can be prevented and your own child will be the one protected from the searing heat.

Lighting the Fuse

Tone of Voice

An argument, like a fire, can start small. A few words, a tone of voice or even a slight threatening action can light the match that gets the fire going. Sarcasm, threat and whining are three voice tones that push other people's hot buttons. Sarcasm belittles a person and an aggressive tone is just as meaningful as an aggressive act. Even a whiny voice can elicit anger by drawing the other person in with its pleading sound. Any voice tone that blames or is accusatory also lights the match of conflict. And a tone that commands or demands usually begets a response that is just as demanding. Are these the sounds that set your co-parent off? Are any of these tones the ones that you respond to with defensiveness or with anger? Tone of voice can carry as much of the message as the actual words. So you can start a fight with your voice even when your words are not the problem.

Body Language

Body language is another way we communicate. And it, too, can be the match that sets an argument burning. Body language can be threatening even when one doesn't push, shove or prevent another's free movement. Jabbing your finger toward someone's face, getting too close by "entering their space," and leaning toward someone in an aggressive manner can all cause someone to ready their fuel for the fight. Even stiff and jerky actions indicate someone's anger and readiness for attack which prepares the other person for counterattacking. Avoiding the other person or withdrawing from a conversation can also light the fuse. Although in some situations it is wise to set limits by withdrawing or removing oneself from a potentially harmful situation, one can also intentionally walk away or ignore a person for the sole purpose of initiating conflict. Body language, the subtle ways we use our body to vent our emotions, is just as likely to start a fight as verbal language and can be even more provocative.

Words That Light Fires

Words themselves carry the third part of the message. Words that . . .

- Blame *(This is all your fault.)*
- Accuse *(You've always hated me.)*
- Demand *(Do not talk to me that way.)*
- Command *(You can't do that.)* . . . are very destructive and ensure that a match is struck.
- Give advice with statements that start, "You should" and "You ought" are also ways to start a conflict.
- Name call often start a fight.
- Psychologize *("You always feel so inferior.")* is a more subtle method of showing off one's superiority.

"You" Statements

If you look at the italicized statements above, you'll notice they have the word "You" in common. They all tell the other person what to do or not do. Since no one likes to be controlled by another person, "You" statements are virtually guaranteed to initiate a conflict. Do you want to start the fire? "You" statements light the fuse.

Fueling the Fire

Strike a match and watch it burn. Does the flame go out or does it grow into a raging fire? The answer depends on how much fuel there is to burn. If there's enough fuel, the fire will build and grow; if not, the little flame quickly goes out. In any argument, if the first comment or body movement doesn't find a reaction, the argument dies out too. If it does and fuel is added in response, the argument grows into a heated exchange.

Your Hot Buttons

How would you respond to these initial comments: You never were good at parenting. You just can't talk rationally. You're always late. You shouldn't stay in that dead-end job of yours. You don't care about our child. Your first response to these lighted matches will determine if more fuel will be thrown on the fire.

Which of the above statements get you hot under the collar? Your own hot buttons allow you to be drawn into an argument. When you're aware of the ones that bother you the most, you can prepare yourself to change your response. You can "take your feet out of the fire." Later in this chapter, you'll learn exactly how to do that, but for now, just become aware of the ways you most easily get drawn into a conflict. Which of the ways that people "Light the Fuse" bother you the most? You already identified your triggers in the previous chapter. Now think of them as your "hot buttons."

Write two or three examples in the spaces below. These are your personal hot buttons.

_____

_____

_____

When someone pushes your hot button it is likely that you will have one of three overreactions:

1) Defensiveness

2) Counterattack

3) Withdrawal

These reactions fuel the fire.

Defensiveness

Your first thoughts perhaps were like these: "I am too a good parent." "I am too able to talk rationally." "I am not always late." "This is not a dead-end job." "I care just as much as you about our child." Defensive, argumentative—these responses get you caught in the fire. When you throw this fuel on the fire, you've allowed someone else to draw you into the fight. Someone else has dangled out a fishing line and you've let yourself get hooked. Someone else has laid a trap and you've gone for the bait and got caught instead.

Counterattack

A second way to walk right into the fire is to counterattack. This is what it sounds like: "Maybe I'm not a perfect parent, but you're worse." "Maybe you think I am irrational, but you're pathetic." "I'm not always on time, but you can't keep up with the child support." "I care about our child more than you do—at least she laughs when she's with me. When she's with you, she's just bored."

There are a thousand ways to counterattack and each one adds fuel to the argument's fire. Counterattack invites further attack, and so the argument builds. The co-parent is caught by entering the trap. The hook is dangled and you grab the bait. Now the fight can really begin. Punch, counterpunch; attack, counterattack. The argument builds; the fire burns brighter. Soon, it's out of control and destruction is all around.

Withdrawal

The third way to fuel the fire is to walk away or hang up on someone. However, there are times when it is appropriate to discontinue a conversation that is nonproductive or abusive. When your children are present or within ear shot, it is not only appropriate, but also important to discontinue hostile interactions. To determine when it is appropriate to limit or discontinue a discussion, simply consider your motive. If you withdraw to push you co-parent's "hot buttons", or because you are unable or unwilling to address an issue, your behavior is sure to fan the flames. When your co-parent does not know why you are withdrawing from a conversation, it is likely that they will assume you are intentionally engaging in a power move. Therefore, be sure to read page 136 to gain a clear understanding of the differences between withdrawing to set limits and withdrawing to invite conflict.

Each of these reactions are very dangerous and negatively influence effective communication. However, under stress they are likely to occur. You will know when you have used one of these reactions because you will suddenly find yourself in a conflicted interaction. As you learn new fire prevention skills you will be able to block your natural responses that fuel the fire.

You might ask yourself, How did this happen? You're both surprised by the size of the flames. You didn't even want a fight. You didn't go looking for it. It couldn't have been that silly little comment that caused the end result. You're sure that the one who threw the fuel on the fire is really the one to blame. But wait, you say. You didn't start it; you were just minding your own business when your co-parent walked right up and pushed your hot button.

It's obvious by now that neither is solely to blame; it takes both the match and the fuel to start the fire. And some behaviors can light the fuse as well as fuel the fire. **Both of you are equally responsible for every argument.** It couldn't have happened without you.

And that's good news. Because that means that <u>**either one of you**</u> **can extinguish the flame.** Either one can stop the fight when you know how. The rest of this chapter will show you how it can be done. You don't have to be caught in the trap. You don't have to be stuck in the burning building. You'll learn how you can defuse any argument and take control of conflict.

Fire Prevention

The first way to limit the fire's destruction is to prevent it before it starts. This doesn't mean that you never say the wrong thing or look the wrong way. It does mean that you minimize danger by not lighting matches in drought-stricken forests.

 **It does mean using the 3 W's:
the When, Where and What guidelines.**

When

Conflict can often be prevented by carefully choosing when to talk. Call to make an appointment. Then both of you can choose a time that's convenient and one when you can limit any distractions. Choose a time when you're well rested and not at the end of a long, tiring day. Select a time when children aren't within earshot so that you can discuss issues freely. Find a mutually agreed upon time when neither one is caught off guard. The beginning or end of transitions is not the time for discussion of other topics.

Where

Next, choose a place conducive to good discussion. You might choose a public place that encourages rational conversation and brings out businesslike behavior. A place where children won't overhear the conversation is also important unless your conflict is firmly under control.

What

Selecting the topic is your next decision. Some topics are out of bounds; some are within limits. It may depend on your goal.

Goal: To air your opinion.

If your goal is to air your opinion, then any topic that impacts your child is within your boundaries. However, you need to be sure that your goal is just to offer your opinion and not to force or persuade your co-parent to share the same opinion. You may prefer your co-parent to share your opinion and believe the result is in your child's best interests, but you can't control your co-parent's reaction. You may want to explain why you believe a TV show is unhealthy for your child, but your co-parent may still choose to follow a different course of action within his/her own house.

Goal: To set your own boundaries.

If your co-parent is infringing on your own choices, you may need an opportunity to set your boundaries. You can ask for a meeting to firmly explain your limits. Here's one example: Your co-parent provides child support for the children. Lately your co-parent has been interfering in the way you spend the money, both advising you and your child as to how the funds should be spent. You call a meeting and firmly but unemotionally explain your limits to this action: You are responsible for the managing the funds and you tell your co-parent that you will no longer require his or her well-meaning advice.

Goal: To solve a problem.

The third kind of goal involves child-related problems that need to be solved. Perhaps the child's grades have dropped or his behavior at school is a problem. Maybe her athletic schedule requires new demands or his use of the car needs some common decisions. When the solution aims to improve the child's life (rather than the parent's position), it's usually a topic for common discussion.

To ensure successful discussions, use the guidelines of The 3 P's.

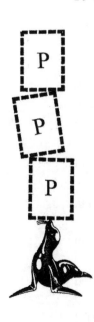

- **Focus on the present, not the past.** Any mention of problems or habits in the past is a sure way to start a defensive argument, so avoid it. Start every new discussion with a clean sheet of paper expecting the current discussion to go well.

- **Focus on the problem, not on the person.** Keep talking about safety issues, and homework conditions rather than "the things you allow at your house." Use language that talks about what's good for the child rather than what you don't like about the co-parent. The problem is the problem. Keep the problem at the center of the discussion and the child at the center of the solution.

- **Focus on the one problem at hand, not the whole universe.** Don't try to change the world. Ask for an appointment to discuss a single topic. And discuss only that topic. When the conversation moves away from the topic, say, "Yes, that's important too, but right now let's focus on this topic." If you succeed in handling one topic, stop. Don't keep talking until you have an argument. Allow yourselves to experience success and enjoy it. If you always push for another topic until you get caught in an argument, you're cheating yourself and your child.

As a summary, fill in the blanks.

Focus on the P . . . . .not the P . . . .

Focus on the P . . . . .not the P . . . .

Focus on one P . . . . .not the universe.

Avoid Playing With Matches

We said that most arguments start with just a tone of voice, a shift of body language, a few words that push another person's hot buttons. How can you honestly reveal what's on your mind and yet avoid playing with matches that set off the fire of conflict?

Avoid making "You" statements. Anytime a sentence starts with the word "You," as in You should . . ., You ought to . . ., You need to . . ., You must . . . or You are (lazy, stupid, silly, a perfectionist, a snob, a jerk, a bum), the speaker is subtly starting an attack. These statements invite either defensiveness or counterattacks and ensure that a battle will ensue. They are tricks to engage the co-parent in a disagreement. They hook the co-parent in the argument and trap him or before she even knows what happened.

If you are to avoid destructive conflict which harms your child, then it's important to realize you start a fight with every "You" statement you make.

Avoid setting up communication barriers. Most "You" statements set up communication barriers. The words that follow the "you" often criticize, blame, insult or interrogate. Let's see why each is a problem.

- **Words that criticize, blame, or accuse** (*You're so lazy; You don't care about our child; You're selfish*) are barriers because they're judgmental, telling the other person what's wrong with him or her. They harm a person's self-esteem and positive sense of himself. When someone's self-esteem has been attacked, the natural reaction is to defend himself or to counterattack. In either case, the focus on the child is lost.

- **Words that advise, command or demand** (*You ought to; You should; You have to*) tell people what to do and put the person in the position of a child, incapable of thinking for herself. That too tears at a person's self-esteem and invites rebellion or revenge.

- **Words that insult** harm a person's self-respect and invite revenge to set the balance right.

- **A series of questions that interrogate** (*What did you do. . . ? And then what happened? What did you do after that?*) are attempts to discover what action a person did wrong. The person being interrogated will soon start protecting himself or start fighting off the inquisition.

- **Words that tell people why they do what they do** are called psychologizing. (*You just can't be assertive because your mother used to hit you whenever you stood up for yourself.*) They may be insightful

122

but they leave a person vulnerable and the speaker in a position of superiority. (I know something you don't know.) And so, like the other "You" statements above, they instigate defensiveness as the person protects his or her self-esteem.

Tone of Voice

Tone of voice by itself can

insult
criticize
demand

It can also relay

sarcasm
aggression
disrespect

If the tone of voice is disrespectful, it forces someone to go on the attack or on the defensive until they've regained their equality. If the person is in a one-down position, he won't communicate until he feels that once again he's on an equal footing. And he won't be able to surrender to another person's request until the position is righted. So using a tone of voice to put someone down or threaten only delays the time that they'll be able to solve a problem or change a course of action that's hurting their child. It directs the focus to the relationship between the two people and away from the problem at hand. It prevents any focus staying on the child.

Body Language

Most of us were never taught anything about how we communicate through body language. However, it's been shown that we communicate as much or more of the message through our body movements and facial expressions as we do through our words. This is often why children are so in tune to the real situation even though parental words tell a different story. A disapproving look, rolling eyes, an aggressive body stance can start a fight just as easily as an insulting remark.

To avoid playing with matches, it's important to start monitoring your own body mechanics and becoming aware of those minor actions that disrupt communication. If the wrong words, tone of voice and body mechanics can start an argument, then the right words, tone of voice and body language can avoid one. If it's your own child who's asleep upstairs when the fire starts, ask yourself if it's worth the effort to avoid playing with matches.

Playing with matches can seem like an exciting and risky venture. However, the result is a loss of focus on the child and the chance that everyone will get burned. Even if you're committed to never starting a fire, you need to know how to replace offending words and actions with ones that are less provocative. We'll focus on what to do in the remainder of this chapter.

Throwing Fuel on the Fire

The match is lit; you're feeling the heat. How do you respond? Do you imagine the worst and consider every statement an attack? Do you intentionally ignore the question and leave the area? Do you lurch toward defending yourself? (I am not always late!) Do you launch a counterattack? (Even when I'm on time, you never have Alex ready!) Remember that any of these comebacks add fuel to the fire. They all turn your co-parent's initial words, tone of voice or look into a full-fledged argument. One person can't argue alone.

When you feel the fire and respond by defending yourself or attacking back, you've agreed to join the fight. You've accepted the invitation to argue. You've agreed to put aside your focus on the child in order to take up arms and join the battle. You've decided that entering the fray is so important to you that you leave your child to fend for himself while you go off to fight your own fights.

How Do You Defuse Conflict?

You've seen the flame and felt its intense heat—maybe under your own collar. Your body says, "Prepare for attack." Now what? STP-A! STOP. THINK. PAUSE: What's in my child's best interest? Remind yourself that fires burn. Resolve to extinguish the flame. Now you're ready to take ACTION.

1. STP-A (Stop . . . Think . . . Pause . . . Act)

2. Take action to control your voice tone
Keep it cool and collected. Take a breath and relax your jaw so that you can control your voice. Your response may be friendly and firm but prevent it from being charged with sarcasm or anger. You can show that you're still in control and you're not willing to let your co-parent control you. Keep your tone even as you respond and your co-parent will focus on your actual words. This action alone can extinguish the flame and put out the fire completely.

3. Take action to control your body movements
Your body language sends a message as powerfully as your tone of voice or the words you speak. When you release your first breath, let your shoulders relax and your jaw slacken slightly. You'll feel better yourself as this stress is released. You'll also find that you now feel in control of the situation. You'll visibly demonstrate that you refuse to be controlled by someone else. You'll show that you are firmly in control of yourself, your body and mind and that you won't be jerked around by someone else's string. You'll decide how you want to act, and you'll want to stay calm in order to solve a problem, discuss an issue or share an opinion.

4. Remove yourself
At times you'll notice how difficult it is to get control of your body, your words or your tone of voice. If you sense that you're losing control, remove yourself from the situation. You may need time and distance away from the situation to regain control of yourself. If you're face-to-face, say that you need time to get yourself together and with a calm voice and unhurried actions remove yourself physically from the situation. Just leave. (This is different from leaving the situation with intentional plans to escalate the argument because to walk away without a word would push your co-parent's hot buttons.)

If the co-parent is aggressive or threatening in any way, you should leave immediately before the argument escalates further. Even if you are both in your house, quietly gather your keys and your child and leave. Don't yank your child by the arm hurriedly; if you do, you escalate the argument through your body mechanics and you increase your child's fear and stress.

You can also remove yourself from telephone conversations that build toward an argument. With the calmest voice possible, say something like, "This isn't doing us much good. I'm hanging up now and I will call you tomorrow." Than calmly hang up. There is no excuse for staying on the phone when an argument starts. If you do, you are acknowledging that you've lost sight of your child's needs and are only there to get revenge for yourself. In the long run, you'll both be hurt.

5. Listen and Reflect

When your co-parent has handed you a lighted match, your job is to put out the fire. There's an image that comes out of the 1970s that's useful to consider. When Vietnam demonstrators were confronted by their own national guardsmen, several put flowers in the barrels of the guardsmen's rifles. What do you think was the effect? National guardsmen could not easily turn their firepower on young men and women armed with flowers. It took the fire out of their bellies, so to speak. Let's see how this applies to co-parents.

When a co-parent drops a "You" statement on you, listen between the lines for the concern hidden there and reflect the concern back to the speaker. For example, "You're not good at parenting" can be reflected back as, "You're concerned that I won't make good decisions concerning our son." Reflecting doesn't mean that you agree with the speaker or even with the concern behind the speaker's statement. And it doesn't mean that you defend your position. A reflective statement only rephrases what the speaker believes and shows you're listening. Let's see some other examples.

"You're always late," can be reflected by saying, "You're unhappy when I arrive later than scheduled."

"You should leave that dead-end job," can be reflected by saying, "You're concerned that I can't progress in this job."

Even a statement like "You're really a jerk" can be reflected with "You don't like the way I make decisions," or "You don't agree with the way I lead my life."

Reflecting statements won't immediately end a confrontation. It may take some winding down with your reflecting back three or four consecutive statements made by the speaker. But it will immediately reduce the level of the conflict because reflecting shows that you are carefully listening to the speaker's underlying concerns. If you can help identify the concern, you may be able to extinguish the flame. Everybody likes being listened to and understood. As author of *"Seven Habits of Highly Effective People,"* Stephen Covey says, "They don't care how much you know until they know how much you care." Show your understanding of the other person's concern and then, even if you disagree, you'll have that person's respect.

6. "I" Statements

"You" statements are like a first attack. In turn, they invite defensiveness or a counteroffensive. Either way they're guaranteed to start an argument. How do you share your opinions, your thoughts or respond to someone else without using a "you" statement? Instead of starting a sentence with "You," start it instead with "I."

This is what it looks like:

"I feel/felt _____	(insert feeling word)
when _____	(this happens)
and what I'd like is _____	(insert your request)"

This is what it sounds like:

"I feel angry when you let our son watch R-rated movies, and what I'd like is for you to leave him with me when you want to go to an adult movie."

"I feel worried when Tasheka comes home smelling of smoke and what I'd like is for you to consider smoking outside."

"I am concerned when I see how depressed Alex is and what I'd like is for us to discuss her seeing a therapist."

These "I" Statements help the communication process in three ways:

- They honestly describe how you feel about a situation. Since feelings are always acceptable (even when actions are not), the statements themselves are more likely to be acceptably received.
- They quickly connect your thoughts about the situation to the possible effect on the child. They can be child-focused. Therefore the discussion is more likely to focus on what's best for the child.
- They don't invite defensiveness or counterattack. Instead, they allow for a respectful difference of opinion and a sharing of ideas. By not forcing someone to take an opposing position, they open the door to mutual agreement.
- They make a brief and clear request.

Full "I" Statement

At times, to give a more complete picture, a full "I" statement is needed rather than the shorter "I" statement mentioned above. Full "I" statements follow this format:

I feel _____(insert feeling word),

when _____(insert what happens that concerns you)

because _____(the negative affect it has on the child).

And what I'd like is _____(your requested change in the behavior).

Can you agree to _____(this request)?

Example #1.

I feel worried when Dwayne is home alone after 9 pm, because he's unprotected and something could happen to him.

I would like him to have a baby-sitter if he's going to be alone after 9:00.

Can you agree to that?

Example #2.

> I feel concerned when Alison doesn't do her homework at your house, because she needs structure in both homes or she may not pass her subjects. And what I'd like is for you to monitor her work.
>
> What do you think of the idea?

The "I" statement helps to keep the problem focused on the child. It clearly changes the focus from what "I" want to what's good for the child.

The last question invites agreement or commitment. However, don't expect agreement immediately. It may take a little time for your co-parent to agree. Don't press for an answer right after you've delivered the "I" statement. Your co-parent may need to say, "I'll think about it," even if he/she agrees in order to save face. Follow up by saying, "Great. I'll call you on Friday to find out what you're thinking."

You can also use an "I" statement when you need to set boundaries. This is what that sounds like:

> I feel hurt and angry when you call me irresponsible. What I'd like is for you to only give me constructive criticism but <u>never</u> in front of our child.
>
> Will you do that?

Dual Responsibility

You can start an argument. You can stop one from developing. Avoid playing with matches by controlling your own tone of voice, words and body language. Keep clear of your co-parent's hot buttons; you know which ones they are.

If an argument does get started, avoid throwing fuel on the fire. Instead, use STP-A to stop and think about the effect on your child if you enter the fray. Then, rather than defending yourself or starting a counteroffensive, listen to the speaker and reflect back his or her hidden concerns. An "I" statement delivered with controlled voice and body mechanics keeps the focus on the needs of your child and limits the size and number of conflicts. You'll keep yourself and your child out of the burning building.

"I" STATEMENTS LOG

Tips for Creating "I" Statements

1. Use the list of feeling words on the following page to help you identify your feelings.

2. When you use the words *like*, *that*, and *as if* after you state "I feel," you will be expressing a thought or a belief rather than an emotion. By using these words you run the risk of lighting the fuse because you may communicate a judgment. The other person may be tempted to counterattack to defend herself against your perceived judgment. Although no one has the right to criticize your feelings, thoughts and judgments are fair game. Attempt to accurately identify your feelings and include them in your communication.

For example:

Don't Say: **I feel *like* you never appreciate what I do. (thought)**
<u>Say:</u>   I feel <u>unappreciated</u> when my efforts go unnoticed. (expression of feeling)

Don't Say: **I feel *that* you should increase the child support now that you have a new job. (judgment)**
<u>Say:</u>   I feel <u>overwhelmed and resentful</u> when I see how financially comfortable you are while I live paycheck to paycheck and what . . . (expression of feelings)

Don't Say: **I feel *as* if you don't care about how badly our daughter looks. (thought or assumption)**
<u>Say:</u>   I feel <u>embarrassed</u> when she is dressed so shabbily because . . . (expression of feeling)

Directions: During the next week record two "I" statements that you used with your co-parent. Be brief and to the point. The goal is to include all the parts of an "I" statement in one or two sentences.

I feel/felt _____

when _____

because _____

and what I'd like is _____

I feel/felt _____

when _____

because _____

and what I'd like is _____

DESCRIPTIVE FEELINGS

Directions: Post this list somewhere you and your child can see it, such as on your refrigerator. Practice identifying your feelings in front of your child and encourage your child to do the same. As you develop your feelings vocabulary, add other feelings words to this list.

FEELING WORDS LIST

PLEASANT FEELINGS			UNPLEASANT FEELINGS		
alive	amused	accepted	annoyed	afraid	anxious
affectionate	alert	adequate	agitated	angry	aggressive
assured	blest	brave	aggravated	abused	blue
bold	buoyant	cocky	bitter	betrayed	bored
cheerful	content	caring	confused	crushed	down
calm	casual	confident	distracted	disappointed	dissatisfied
capable	competent	encouraged	depressed	disgruntled	exhausted
empathetic	expectant	excited	envious	embarrassed	frustrated
energetic	ecstatic	fascinated	frightened	hurt	helpless
fortunate	fine	friendly	horrible	hopeless	insecure
glad	determined	great	infuriated	ill	incompetent
good	goofy	gutsy	irritated	livid	lost
hopeful	happy	high	miffed	mean	nervous
humble	joyful	intense	outraged	offended	provoked
important	loving	optimistic	possessive	pushed	peeved
overjoyed	playful	peaceful	putout	rage	rejected
pleased	proud	positive	remorse	resentful	stunned
powerful	relaxed	refreshed	shaky	stupid	sullen
relieved	sincere	secure	sad	spiteful	tense
silly	satisfied	snappy	ticked off	timid	tired
snappy	surprised	sympathetic	trapped	unamused	useless
successful	sassy	thankful	uneasy	vengeful	inadequate
thrilled	warm & fuzzy	wonderful	worn	worried	weary

TAKING CONTROL OF CONFLICT

Directions: Read the dos and don'ts below. Put an "x" on the behaviors in the right-hand column that you practice which add fuel to the fire. Circle the behaviors in the left-hand column that you need to practice.

DO Defuse the Fire	DON'T Fuel the Fire
• Use self control	Respond before you think
• Breathe	Threaten
• Watch your tone	Criticize
• Watch your body language	Counterattack or Blame
• Use STP-A	Defend
• Listen to the co-parent	Use sarcasm
• Stay "child-focused"	Stay "self-focused"
• Reflect what you heard	Demand or Command
• Use "I" Statements	Use "You" Statements
• Use the 3 W's	Use words like "always" and "never"
• Use facts & observations	Use judgments
• Stay present-focused	Stay past-focused
• Address only one issue at a time	Change subjects or distract
• If necessary ask to speak later and set a time	Use the words "should" and "always"
• If necessary set limits	Interrogate
• If necessary leave or hang up phone	Psychologize or analyze
(Announce first that you are leaving, etc.)	Use name-calling, labeling or swearing
• Use businesslike skills	Ignore or withdraw
• Use 7 negotiating skills	Focus on winning
• Empathize: Find something to agree or relate to	Dominate the conversation

IT'S YOUR CHOICE . . . YOU DECIDE

'LIGHTING THE FUSE'
HOSTILITY + HOSTILITY = GREATER HOSTILITY

Directions: Read the following examples and predict the possible outcome. Then take each situation and attempt to be the responding parent. Create a better outcome by de-escalating the conflict. Use the do's and don'ts listed on the activity page titled "Taking Control of Conflict" as your guide.

Example #1.

Mother: 'Why can't you ever get our daughter home on time? I always have to be the responsible one! I think you run late on purpose just to annoy me. You are so passive-aggressive! You must enjoy making us rush at bedtime!"

Father: "Right, YOU'RE the responsible one! Ha! What a laugh. You can't even balance your checkbook! Get off my back. I'll get her home when I can! You always like to control things, don't you?"

Identify the ways the father chose to create greater hostility:

_____

_____

_____

_____

Using your skills, take the role of the father, and DEFUSE the above situation.

Father:

_____

_____

_____

_____

Example #2

Father: "You're trying to make trouble aren't you? You know the courts said you are to provide the children's clothes with the huge child support check you get from me, but NO, you continue to send the kids with nasty, ugly, inappropriate clothes! Don't you care about how they look? I can't believe the games you play just to get back at me for wanting the divorce!"

Mother: "What are you complaining about? I send clothes. The judge didn't say what kind of clothes they had to be. You should be happy with what I send. And besides you didn't return the nice stuff I used to pack. If you don't like it, buy more clothes. You're the one with all the money anyhow. And remember the divorce was your fault, so why deny it? If it weren't for your trashy little secretary, we'd still be together!"

Identify ways the mother increased the hostility:

_____

_____

_____

_____

Using your skills, take the role of the mother and DEFUSE the above situation.

Mother:

_____

_____

_____

_____

_____

DEFUSE WITH "I" STATEMENTS

Directions: Read the examples and convert them to "I" statements. Use the format

"I feel _____

When _____

Because _____

And what I'd like is _____."

1. "I can't believe you! You promised you would be on time for a change, and you forgot again! I can't trust you to do anything right!"

_____

_____

_____

_____

2. "You are so darn controlling! I can't believe what you are doing to the children. You are not supposed to pump them for information about me or my boyfriend! Just because you are jealous and lonely, don't take it out on the poor kids! If you don't stop doing stuff like this, I'll call my attorney!"

_____

_____

_____

_____

3. "You took our child to see a therapist?! Are you crazy? There is nothing wrong with my son! Well, nothing other than having to deal with a crazy mother! Just because you need treatment doesn't mean he does! I want the name of that therapist so I can put a stop to this foolishness! I don't want him thinking there is something wrong with him. You don't have the right to make this kind of decision without me!"

---

4. "I can bring my boyfriend Fred over anytime I want. You can't tell me who the children can be around. They need a positive male role model and Fred is wonderful. But I guess you wouldn't know anything about that, would you? Besides the kids really like him! They can tell HE makes me happy. We act like a family and you can't stop us!"

---

5. "I am not going to send good clothes anymore because you will not ever return them!. You are just playing games again. The judge said you are to stop these maneuvers."

_____

_____

_____

_____

_____

_____

6. "You won't ever answer the phone when I call. I know you have caller ID and I bet you are standing there pretending you are not home. Why can't I just talk to my kids?!"

_____

_____

_____

_____

_____

DEFUSE WITH LIMITS
Review Page

When to set limits with your co-parent:

- To protect yourself from an uncomfortable or unsafe situation

- To end a discussion that is deteriorating or continually off the topic

- To protect your child from experiencing parental conflict or tension

How to set limits:

- Use an "I" statement to request a change in volume, behavior, etc.

- Ask to continue the conversation later and offer a date and time

- Tell the co-parent in clear and specific language what behaviors you will not tolerate. Then stand behind your words and remove yourself from the situation if the behaviors of the co-parent do not change.

- Use the above behaviors to set limits on the phone. When the co-parent does not respond to the limits, do the next five steps immediately:

1. Announce that you are getting off the phone

2. Offer a time to "try again"

3. Do **not** wait for agreement

4. Gently hang up the phone

5. Call them back when you agreed to

As with any limits, they will mean absolutely nothing if you do not follow through.

DEFUSE WITH LIMITS ACTIVITY

Directions: Rewrite each of the comments to reflect limit-setting behaviors and statements.

1. "I hate when you start yelling at me when I am dropping off our daughter. Can't you see how upset you are making her? Please don't do this; don't be difficult. Please, please... just stop yelling at me!"

2. "You called to talk to Jeffrey, so why are you always asking to talk to me? I've told you before that I don't want to talk with you! Please don't put him into the middle. No, I don't want to discuss that either. Why are you pushing this?"

3. "He is coming home with me; it's supposed to be my day anyhow! What do you mean he can't come with me? How dare you! He is coming with me right now, so get out of our way! Don't try to stop me!" (You grab your child from the other parent. Your child looks anxious and confused. Your child begins to cry).

Dear Mom and Dad,

I think it's really great that you are learning to talk to each other without fussing so much. Now I don't have to worry every time I see you both together! I'm even going to learn from you, so keep up the good work! It's never too late to learn how to communicate! Thanks.

Your excited kid!

XXXXXOOOOOXXXXX

Chapter Six Review

1. Using the fire analogy explain why it takes two people to create a conflict.

2. Explain why it only takes one person to stop a conflict.

3. What happens if a spark receives no fuel?

4. Name a few ways in which you fuel the fire?

5. What are the three primary "reactions" that can fuel a fire?

6. What are the three "W's" and how do they facilitate conversations?

7. What are the three "P's" and how will they help you communicate with your co-parent?

8. What will you do to defuse conflict in the future?

9. What is the value of "reflecting?"

10. How will using "I Statements" help you to communicate?

11. Explain why the following are not "I-statements."

    I feel as if you
    I feel that you
    I feel like you

12. When is it productive and wise to use limits? Explain why limits may actually light the fuel? If you need to remove yourself from a conversation, what should you do first?

7.

All a Winner or Winner Take All

Negotiating Agreements

7.

Negotiating Agreements
(All a Winner or Winner Take All)

"I'm glad you could come in today," the teacher says to Sam's parents, Jim and Sarah. "As I said on the phone, Sam is having some serious problems that we need to discuss. His behavior is not only interfering with his own progress, but is interrupting his classmates' work too."

When the teacher pauses before describing the problem in detail and offering her suggestions for solving it, the co-parents initiate their own discussion:

"If you hadn't walked out on us, he wouldn't be having this problem now," Sarah begins to wail.

"You don't see the forest for the trees, do you?" Jim retaliates. "You're so quick to assign blame, you don't even wait to hear out the problem."

Who Really Wins?

TIME OUT! Who do you think is winning this argument? While it may be unclear who's winning, what is perfectly clear is that the child is the sure loser. He's got a problem, but the parents' continuing conflict prevents their finding a solution. The effort the parents could be using to solve the problem is deflected, instead, toward winning the fight. What happens then is that the focus moves from the child's problem and to the parents' self-interest. Remember Chapter One: being "Child-Focused" is the goal.

Each time one parent tries to win at the other's expense, it's like winning the battle but losing the war. The battle is the immediate parental disagreement; the war is the long-term development of their child.

Remember the long-term goal, raising a happy and well adjusted child, is the primary reason that the two adults continue their relationship. With their common goal in mind, they should declare themselves winners only if they solve problems in a way that satisfies their child's best interests. When they fail to achieve that goal and instead get sidetracked on making the co-parent the loser, then everyone, including the parents and their child, loses.

That's why the title of this chapter is "All a Winner or Winner Take All." In post-divorce parenting, *if either parent wins at the other's expense then everyone loses.* The only way for a parent to win is to make the child the clear winner. Then, regardless of which parent wins or loses the immediate argument, they are all winners in the long-term view.

Let's see how this works: One parent has all the financial security; the other falls into poverty. Who wins? The child can't escape the part of her life spent in poverty. The wealthier parent wins the financial argument and keeps most of the money; but the child loses the war by experiencing poverty's dangerous side effects. In the long term, they both lose.

If winning is defined as finding the solution that is best for the child, then every problem has a solution acceptable to both parents. Co-parents now become collaborators who solve problems rather than **adversaries who make problems**. When you find the best solution for your child, then you can say, "I've won."

Typical Problems

Post-divorce parents share several common problems. These problems occur frequently in post-divorce situations; some require a negotiated settlement. That does not mean they require a court settlement; it means that they may need strategic problem-solving in order to get to a negotiated co-parent agreement. Common problems include the ones listed below.

Problems Commonly Requiring Negotiated Solutions in Post-divorce Parenting

Schedules

Extracurricular activities

Religion

Choice of doctor

Bedtime

Food selection

Public vs. private school

Selection of college

Value-Laden

You'll see that many of these topics are value-laden. They may have deeper meaning attached to them than the surface issue. For example, the a child's bedtime may have more to do with the parent's own time-management, rigidity with rules and comfort with routines than with the child's need for sleep.

Acceptance of Differences

It may be hard for co-parents to realize that all people have differences. It's what makes us unique and our lives interesting. We all see life through a filtered lens built out of our own personal experiences and value systems. Therefore any two people will bring differing opinions and perceptions into a discussion of decisions or problems requiring solutions. However, the threat to children in post-divorce families is that the opinions solidify into positions. Then parents start fighting to maintain their positions rather than concentrate on solving the child's problem.

It's important to remain the unique person you are, but to commit to placing the highest priority on finding a workable solution that meets the child's needs. This will mean that you won't always get what you want. That's a given. But that's the price you pay for having a healthy child. That's the decision you have to make. You have to accept that if you win and "take all" your child loses. Instead you have to make finding the best solution to keep everyone a winner your ultimate goal.

Steps to Negotiating Agreements

Once a commitment is made to finding a solution, you can follow a seven-step method for finding the best solution and putting it into effect. These are the steps and the guidelines for using them effectively in real-life situations.

Step 1
Name the Problem

How do you know when there's a problem to solve? One of the co-parents will perceive that there is a problem interfering with the well-being of the child. Or he or she becomes aware that a change in the child's life could offer some improvement. For example, a change in the method of transition could reduce the child's stress. Or a change in the schedule will allow the child to see his or her grandparents. Or an agreement between the co-parents on bedtime will improve the child's attitude during the day. Or one co-parent receives the message from the child's teacher that he or she is having vision or behavioral problems in school.

The co-parent who first becomes aware of the problem should be the one to call the other co-parent in order to make an appointment for resolving the problem. This is where the "fire prevention" or conflict prevention guidelines that we discussed in the last chapter come into play.

- **WHEN:** Call for a meeting when both co-parents are free from distraction and when the child will not overhear the discussion.

- **WHERE:** Hold the meeting with the co-parent where both are likely to be on their best businesslike behavior. Hold the meeting where the child is not able to overhear the conversation.

- **WHAT:** Call the meeting to discuss a single topic, one that is clearly in the best interest of the child.

Guidelines for Step 1: Name the Problem

Remember the communication guidelines from the last chapter when naming the problem. Use an "I" statement or describe the situation with facts or observations. Here are some examples:

- "I'm concerned when Jamie gets home from the weekend and he can't seem to go to bed at his usual time. Then he can't get up for school on Monday. I'd like to see if we can work out a bedtime schedule that works for him all the time."

- "I have a business conflict that will take me out of town next weekend. I'd like to reschedule my weekend with Shawn."

- "I'm worried because Kelly's teacher called to say that she's having some problems in school. What I'd like is to go together and find out what we can do to help."

IGNITING THE FUSE

Remember, the way you describe the problem has the potential for igniting a fuse. If you use a voice tone that's critical or demanding, body language that is disrespectful or threatening, or words that blame or criticize, you'll decrease the chances of finding a solution. *(Example: "John isn't getting his homework done. He's lazy, just like you.")* Instead, you'll ensure that your child's problem continues. Keep the communication principles from the last chapter in mind when you raise the problem or voice your concern.

SAMPLE SITUATION

Robert and Jackie have a daughter named Rachel. Robert picks Rachel up each Friday night at 6:00 PM. However, he generally calls Jackie from his office informing her that he will be late to pick up Rachel. Typically, the parents exchange insults and end up in an argument. Jackie is determined to solve the problem. On a previous attempt, Jackie tried an "I" statement to let Robert know what she wanted from him. However, the problem hasn't been solved. Robert is still between 15 minutes and an hour late every Friday. Now, Jackie is going to bring up the problem again. If you were Jackie how would you describe the problem to Robert?

STEP 1.

_____

_____

_____

SAMPLE: I'm anxious and concerned when Rachel doesn't get picked up on time on Friday nights. I'm concerned that Rachel is worried about you not coming and I get anxious because I know I'll be late to meet with my friends. And when I get stressed out, I worry that my stress adds to Rachel's stress. I'd like to find a solution to this problem that works for both of us.

Step 2
Give opinion; Reflect opinion

Step 2 is perhaps the most critical step in moving from the problem to the solution. When this step isn't handled carefully, the conversation becomes refocused on the relationship between the co-parents rather than staying focused on solving the child's problem. *This step is the hardest for most parents to follow. It takes commitment to the long-term solution; it takes self-control to put one's emotions aside temporarily; it takes self-discipline to use an unfamiliar skill.*

This is what you do: The co-parents take turns giving their opinions as to how they perceive the problem or how the problem affects them. Immediately following the expressed opinion, the other co-parent reflects the words expressed by the first co-parent.

It sounds like this:

(1) Jackie gives an opinion; Robert reflects Jackie's opinion

Jackie's opinion: **"When you're late picking up Rachel, I'm late for meeting my friends. I feel stressed out and may be passing on that concern to Rachel."**

Robert reflects: **"You get anxious when you can't plan on a regular time for making plans with friends on Friday nights."**

(2) Robert gives an opinion; Jackie reflects Robert's opinion

Now the other parent has a turn to express his opinion and have his opinion reflected.

Robert's opinion: **"I have a hard time knowing when I can leave work on Friday nights. Leaving at a specific time puts extra pressure on me since there are often details that I can't walk away from. I don't want to cause either you or Rachel to be upset."**

Jackie reflects: **"You feel stressed by having to leave work at a specified time when some things aren't finished. You would like to solve the problem so that you don't have extra pressure and Rachel and I don't have extra stress."**

Guidelines for Step 2: Give Opinion; Reflect Opinion

Reflecting the co-parent's opinions require that you put aside your own opinions and emotions temporarily. You need to listen to the co-parent's thoughts and feelings, then put the person's opinions into your own words. Try not to add to or subtract from the message delivered by the co-parent. The more accurate your description, the better the chances are that you'll solve the problem.

Secondly, remember you don't have to agree with the person's thoughts or feelings. For example, should one parent say that he thinks vegetarian foods are healthier for the child, you can reflect the content of the message by saying, "You believe that a vegetarian diet is a healthy diet," and still remain a meat-eater yourself.

The purpose of this step is for each side to have the opportunity to explain his own thinking on the subject fully. Sometimes you might even want to say, "Tell me more about that" if you're confused or don't fully understand the person's concerns or opinions.

Respect for Differences

It's not expected that you and your co-parent will fully agree on every topic. These topics raise issues that strike at our deepest values which, of course, are different for each of us. However, it is still important to demonstrate respect whether or not you agree with the person's opinion. The opportunity to explain one's opinion and state one's values helps both parents clarify their own thinking. Sometimes a parent realizes that the issue is more about being respected than finding agreement and will even back off his position when he knows he's being heard. Other times it helps her realize just how strongly her co-parent cares about an issue and how important it can be to accommodate that person's beliefs, at least partially.

Caution

Remember, reflecting is where the problem can easily turn into an argument. If you respond to the problem by taking it personally, you will fuel the flames and turn the problem into a fight. One way this happens is by reacting defensively when the problem is described: "I'm not giving you or Rachel stress. I'm just trying to do my job." The other way to fuel the flames is by acting like the problem is a personal attack requiring a counterattack.

That would sound like this: "I'm just trying to do my job. You're the one causing Rachel stress when you get so tied to a stupid clock. Can't you lighten up a little?" With each parent expressing his opinion and then having the co-parent reflect it, it is much more likely that they'll stay focused on the child's problem and find a mutually agreeable solution.

Step 3
Brainstorm Solutions

Step 3 is where alternative solutions are proposed. It's very important that you don't judge or evaluate solutions at the same time you're brainstorming potential options. Instead, propose or suggest as many ideas as you can. You can get real crazy here and suggest ideas that you don't like or that sound unusual. When one idea is suggested, try suggesting the opposite idea. By opening your minds up to all kinds of creative solutions, you might come up with an outlandish idea that works better than all the simple solutions you thought of at first.

BRAINSTORM OPTIONS TO THE 'FRIDAY NIGHT' DILEMMA
(Jackie and Robert's Problem)

Robert picks up Rachel at midnight.

Robert picks up Rachel on Saturday.

Jackie picks up Robert.

Robert picks up Rachel when Jackie returns.

Jackie leaves Rachel alone until Robert arrives.

Jackie gets a sitter.

Jackie stays home on Friday nights.

Can you see how few of these provide a good solution but any one of them provides a germ of a potentially great solution? Staying open to ideas without pre-judging them is an absolute must. No one is allowed to say an idea is out of bounds or unacceptable at this stage. If you do, then it prevents other ideas from emerging. A large number of potential ideas will emerge only if people think they won't be rejected for having a stupid idea. Then the ideas will flow more freely and a great idea may be found among them.

Step 4
Choose a Solution

Now is the time to evaluate the proposed solutions and choose the best solution. Remember, the key question to ask is, "What is the best solution for the child?" You might find that you'll even combine some of the proposed solutions and come up with a solution that's even better.

You may also find that you need more information in order to determine the best solution. You may need to ask other people for their input or get a recommendation. You may need to check with other people involved or get other opinions on the effect of a proposed change on the child. It's all right to complete these steps on different days. You don't have to complete steps one through seven in one appointment. Just don't leave this appointment until you've decided when you're going to meet again to complete the next step.

SAMPLE SITUATION

After Jackie and Robert came up with some potential solutions, they started to discuss the ones that looked plausible. In fact, they combined two ideas to make an even better solution.

Jackie: **"So, we've decided that I'll get a sitter to be here from 6:00 on Fridays until you arrive, sometime between 6 and 7 PM."**

Robert: **"That's right. And I'll pay the sitter for one hour even if I'm there at 6:15 PM. You'll tell Rachel that I'll be there before 7 PM so that she won't be worried about my not coming at all. Then I'll take the sitter home when I pick up Rachel."**

Jackie: **"It sounds like a good solution for all of us."**

Step 5
Review Who Does What by When

In the last example we saw Jackie and Robert not only choose the best solution but also review the solution. That means summarizing the agreement in your own words and saying who is responsible for taking which actions. It's a good idea to also name the time when these actions should be completed. This step can prevent a lot of problems later on.

People often hear what they want to hear and then they act on what they thought they heard. Co-parents may not always hear the same information. Therefore, it's important to review the decision, putting into words what was decided and who will carry out which parts of the decision.

This step follows the same principles of a good business relationship: Leaders of good business meetings recap the group's decisions at the conclusion of the meeting and remind everyone of their resulting responsibilities. Use these questions as your guide:

- Which actions are needed to carry out the decision?
- Who is responsible?
- What will the person do in order to fulfill the responsibility?
- When should this action be completed?

By reviewing these guidelines before leaving the appointment, co-parents can prevent miscommunication from happening. You'll prevent the frustration that can occur when there isn't clarity about everyone's responsibilities. Plus you'll head off the "I thought you were going to do that," comment that interferes with the success of the whole process.

Step 6
Put the Solution into Action

Here is where the rubber meets the road, when you put your agreement into action. This is so straightforward that there shouldn't be any problem. Why is there?

Two reasons:

1. A parent is not committed to the solution.
2. A parent forgets about the long-term commitment to his/her child and falls back on the short-term desire to win the battle with co-parent.

Commitment

Commitment is crucial to the long term goal of a healthy upbringing for your child. If your co-parent loses faith in your willingness to carry out your agreements, you put both the co-parent relationship and your child's well-being in jeopardy. A sense of mistrust is extremely damaging to the long-term effectiveness of your parenting.

It is destructive to your child's future relationships when there is not a sense of trust forged early in his life. Relationships thrive on trust and they wither from mistrust. If either your child or your co-parent mistrusts you, the poison emitted will seep into the fabric of your child's trust in others. You are the role model; you demonstrate the way. Whenever you agree to a solution you should carry it through; fulfilling your commitments becomes one of your child's fundamental life supports.

Setting Time Limits

When you are having difficulty agreeing to any of the proposed solutions but you want to support solving the problem, try this idea. Limit the solution to a designated period of time. It might be a few days or a few months, depending on the situation. Be sure to make the specified time period long enough to give the solution a chance to work. That may mean including enough time to adjust to the change. Give it a fair shake so that you can get accurate feedback on how well the solution works.

By setting a designated period of time for trying out the solution, you don't have to put all your eggs in one basket. You may be dragging your feet on agreeing to any proposed solution because you're afraid that you'll have to live with the results forever. If you designate a specific period of time for evaluating the solution in action, you're free to return to the drawing board and renegotiate if the solution isn't working for either you or your child. You don't have to choose the perfect solution the first time; you only have to find a solution that you're willing to try for a limited time. Ask yourself, "Can I live with this for three weeks?" If the answer is yes, then it's a great solution. You've got something to try—and it just might work out for the long term.

A problem is identified. Solutions are brainstormed and an agreement is made. The solution is put into action. Now what?

Now you need to set aside a time to re-evaluate the decision. When you evaluate the solution, ask the following questions: What worked? What didn't? What needs to be changed? Was it a one-time situation or does the solution need to continue on a regular basis? Who benefits from the solution? And most of all, is this solution in the best interest of the child?

Time to Re-evaluate

When you and your co-parent plan to re-evaluate the solution, use your fire prevention (conflict prevention) tactics:

- Designate a time to re-evaluate the solution.
- Either parent can call the meeting.
- Use your communication guidelines (control of the tone of voice, the body language and the words) in order to evaluate the solution to the problem and not cause additional problems.

Follow the same steps as for negotiating the agreement:

1. Either parent can initiate the evaluation.
2. Allow both parents to give their view of how well the solution is working. Reflect the co-parent's point of view.
3. Decide whether you need to brainstorm new solutions or keep the same solution.
4. Choose the best solution (which may be continuing the same action).
5. Review who will do what.
6. Put the new solution into action or continue with the same solution.
7. Re-evaluate.

SUMMARY

Throughout this book, you've been increasing your understanding of good communication and learning skills to put that knowledge into practice. Now you're being called upon to put to use everything you've learned when solving the most difficult challenges in post-divorce parenting: negotiating agreements. When you use these seven steps plus the communication guidelines and skills you've formed by reading this book, you will be on course to win the prize. You may not be the winner who "takes all" but you and your child will be the big winners.

 # Exercises

NEGOTIATING AGREEMENT

Develop a step-by-step process to use as a guide. Outline the steps to negotiating agreement in the spaces provided.

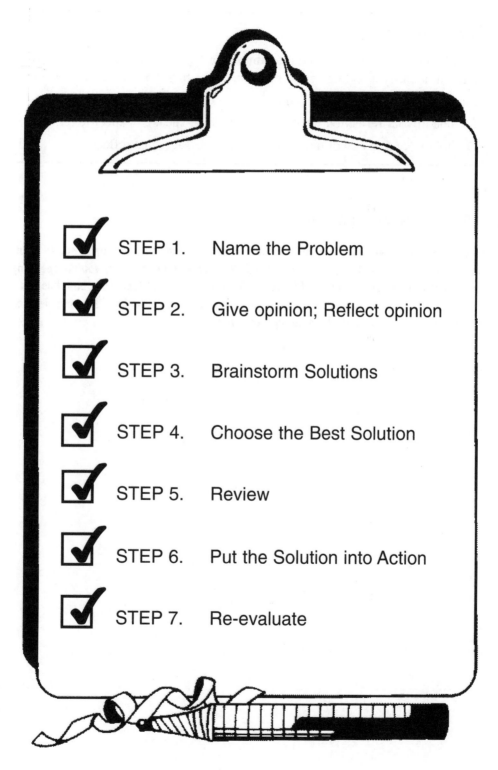

STEP 1.   Name the Problem

STEP 2.   Give opinion; Reflect opinion

STEP 3.   Brainstorm Solutions

STEP 4.   Choose the Best Solution

STEP 5.   Review

STEP 6.   Put the Solution into Action

STEP 7.   Re-evaluate

REFLECTIVE LISTENING PRACTICE

Directions: Read the following example and then summarize what the speaker is saying. Do not add to, or take away from, what they are saying. Remember, when you are reflecting you are not saying that you agree or disagree with what is being said. Lastly, do not fall into the trap of trying to solve the problem— just reflect it.

Tips for Reflective Listening:

- Determine if the speaker used a feelings word to describe his emotions. If he did not, identify a feelings word that represents how you think he is feeling.

- Summarize what the speaker said.

- Include in your reflection what you heard as the speaker's specific request.

- Do not respond to any of the content of the message, just reflect.

Example #1

REFLECTING WHAT YOUR CHILD TELLS YOU

Your child says: **"I hate it when Daddy asks me questions about you and your new boyfriend. He wants to know every time you two are together. He also wants to know how much money you are spending on me. I just don't know what to tell him. If I tell him these things, then I feel really bad, like I'm a spy. But if I don't answer him he gets really angry and tries to make me feel sad for him! He even said that I love you more than him! I hate being divorced!"**

Reflect Back:

_____

_____

_____

_____

_____

_____

_____

Example #2

REFLECTING WHAT YOUR CO-PARENT IS SAYING TO YOU

The co-parent says: **"You NEVER keep your word! You are ALWAYS changing the plans. Don't you care what a poor example you are setting for your son? Don't you care how your behavior makes him feel? He cries when you forget to call or when you change your plans at the last minute. I'm the one who has to pick up the pieces when you hurt him. You are just like your father! Is this what you want? Your son needs for you to be involved and to be dependable. I couldn't make you act like a grown-up when we were married, so I don't know why I expect you to be dependable now."**

Reflect Back: (Remember, do not respond to the negative comments and DO NOT DEFEND YOURSELF, just reflect.)

_____

_____

_____

_____

_____

_____

_____

REFLECTION LOG

Directions: Take the time to reflect at least once during the week with your child or children. Try to also practice with a co-worker or a friend. Then try practicing with your co-parent. Practice as much as you can—developing new skills takes lots of conscious effort. Phone conversations can also be used in this activity. Remember, the more negative information you are hearing the harder it will be to reflect without defending or counterattacking. So practice, practice, practice.

Ask yourself:

- Did I add any of my own thoughts?
- Did I forget any important parts?
- Did my reflecting seem to make the speaker feel heard?
- Did my reflecting "light the fuse?"
- Did my reflecting seem to "defuse the fire?"

DATE	PERSON	REFLECTION (issue)	REACTION

REVISED PARENTAL CONCERNS

Look back to page 18 and 19 where you have been recording your parenting concerns. Mark off any issues that have been resolved. Transfer the remaining parenting concerns to this page. Record them using the "I" statement format.

I feel/felt _____**when** _____**and what I'd like is** _____.

1.

2.

3.

4.

5.

6.

7.

8.

9.

10

Dear Mom and Dad,

I can already see that you are doing better! I know that problems are hard to solve sometimes, but knowing that you are looking out for me helps me feel calmer. Thank goodness. Now I can be just a kid and let you solve all the grown-up problems. Thanks.

Love,

Your playful kid!

XXXXXXXOOOOOOO

Chapter Seven Review

1. Explain what the expression "all a winner" means.

2. Can you identify value differences between you and your co-parent? If so, can you come to either an agreement or acceptance around these differences?

3. Name the seven steps to negotiation.

4. What should you do before you begin to negotiate?

5. Does reflecting mean to "interpret the speaker" or to "respond to the speaker" or neither?

6. Why is it important in reflecting not to add or leave out anything important? When can you share your thoughts and feelings?

7. What is the value of "brainstorming?"

8. What is the value of reviewing the details in step five of the negotiation model?

9. What is the value of setting limits on a solution?

10. What is the purpose of re-evaluating the solution in step seven?

11. Which step do you omit or struggle with and what can you do to improve that skill?

8.

Cooperation or Conflict

Co-Parenting is Forever

8.

Co-Parenting is Forever
(Cooperation or Conflict)

Parenting is Forever

While the marriage bond can be severed, with the two parties going their respective ways, the bond between a parent and child can never be obliterated. When one becomes a parent, one assumes the role for life. Even when the parent doesn't participate in a child's life, the role remains. No one else can fill the role of biological parent. A child still wants to know who his parent is, what the parent looks like, what motivates the person and what makes up the character or personality of the person. A child can love other parents (step-parents or adoptive parents) and those parents can love and nurture a child. However, there is always a special place kept available for the biological parent.

The influence of parents in the wake of a divorce remains enormous. Each parent is uniquely important to the child. Each parent has a separate relationship with the child, and is valued in his or her own way. When a parent is absent or fails to fulfill his important role, there is a void. When a parent is criticized, the child is put under increased stress. Because a child hasn't fully separated himself from his parents, any attack on a parent is experienced as an attack on him, and any absence is experienced like the child's missing a piece of himself.

Divorce is a painful severing of the ties between two married adults. It is not intended to sever the relationship between parent and child. It may seem obvious, but a divorce between adults does not mean a divorce with the children. The value of the continued relationship between parent and child far outweighs any preference one parent might have over the continued relationship between the other co-parent and child.

Keeping the relationship between the child and both parents positive after the divorce is of primary importance. Because of this importance, the term co-parents is used to demonstrate the equal worth of each parent. Having both parents involved with a child after a divorce is not just the *best* option; it's the *only* option that can provide the optimal environment in which a child thrives.

How well that relationship works is key to the child's recovery from the trauma of divorce. The better the relationship between co-parents, the better environment for the child. The worse the relationship between the co-parents, the worse the prognosis for the child's future emotional health.

How well the relationship works is up to you. You have a direct effect on its success or failure. Your words, tone of voice and body language will make the difference. Do you push your co-parent's hot buttons or try to stay clear of them? Are you able to let go of the previous relationship and the hurt associated with it? Are you able to realign your relationship so you work out problems and stay focused on the needs of the child? Or are you caught in a revenge cycle that poisons everything? By yourself you can destroy the chances of a good co-parent relationship. When you are committed to making the co-parent relationship work because of its effect on the child, you have the best chance to make it work.

Chapter 1: Making the Commitment to Caring

The first chapter asks you to override the benefits you may receive from having conflict with your co-parent in order to commit yourself to providing your child with the benefits of limited parental conflict. **Remember, the amount of parental conflict is the single most important influence on your child's recovery from the trauma of divorce.**

Making the commitment to a successful co-parent relationship is not enough, however.

- It also takes a lot of hard work.
- It takes effort to stop yourself from reacting negatively in front of your child.
- It takes strength to consider the child's best interests before you decide an appropriate reaction.
- It takes mental toughness to think of alternatives when you're brainstorming ways to solve problems
- It takes self-control to decide how you will respond when one of your own hot buttons has been pushed.
- It takes emotional strength and renewed vigor to let go of the old pain and to move on to uncertain territory.

Using New Techniques

You can draw from the range of techniques presented here if you are to succeed in your goal to provide the best possible environment for your child's positive emotional health. You will need to arm yourself with the best techniques in your arsenal. Here's a brief review of the techniques presented in this book.

Chapter 2: Allowing My Child to Love Both Parents

In Chapter 2 we talked about the stress of a child caught in the middle. When the child is put in situations where he has to choose sides, the child feels forced to renounce one of his parents. Put-downs, criticisms, name-calling, body language that indicates disapproval of the child's other parent and playing the victim make it virtually impossible for the child to stay neutral. The child is often put into a "loyalty bind."

The increased stress that results from being in the middle of a tug of war causes the child to feel trapped, unable to make the best decision for himself in any situation. He feels guarded and careful, weighing the consequence of every action so that he can protect himself from this position whenever possible. He loses the natural spontaneity that is a child's right.

She also experiences a loss of self-esteem since any attack on the child's parent is experienced much like an attack on the child herself, and her own happiness suffers.

To prevent these negative influences from hurting your child, **you can resolve to keep your child out of loyalty binds.** You will be better able to do this when you consider the value of each parent in a child's life. Focus on the qualities and characteristics that the parent can contribute to parenting in a positive way.

Then take the appropriate actions based on these new beliefs. Your first step is:

• Use the STP-A technique to stop yourself from showing negative reactions to your co-parent's words or deeds. You have to decide when and how you will respond out of range of the child's ears and eyes. This means not criticizing the co-parent in front of the child with words, tone of voice, or body language.

• Secondly, you can take actions which allow the child to love his or her other parent. It's a gift you give your child which allows the child to love himself. Talk about the positive qualities or characteristics the child might have inherited from his other parent or mention a shared interest they might have.

• Thirdly, resolve to keep the child out of the middle. Do not pass notes or verbal communication to your co-parent through your child. Always communicate directly with the co-parent. Minimize the number of times the child has to choose between parents attending a school function or sporting event.

• And, finally, don't burden the child with your own emotional needs. If you play the victim and get the child to side with you out of guilt, the child will later resent you for your obvious manipulation. Meeting your own emotional needs is important, but getting them met through your children is an emotional burden that can harm a child for life.

Chapter 3: Changing My Long-Term Role

This chapter asks you to refocus the relationship you have with the parent of your child by de-emphasizing their relationship as a former spouse and instead emphasizing the relationship as co-parent. To succeed you first must disengage from your former spouse. This means **letting go of the old relationship,** both physically and emotionally. Emotional dependence is indicated by continued participation in revenge cycles. Disengaging means putting the old relationship behind you, grieving and mourning its loss, then getting on with your new life. It means seeing yourself as totally responsible for your future: your economic health, your physical health, and your emotional health.

Chapter 4: Choosing My Personal Path

This chapter asks you to consider if you want to make your life 'better or if you want to be bitter. If you choose to make it better, you will **change the focus of the new relationship by centering it entirely on being parents to your child(ren). Your new relationship will become realigned.** It will exist for the primary purpose of rearing your children in the best possible environment and it asks you to do everything in your power to make it the best environment for a child being reared in two families.

Realignment asks you to accept the new family structure which is housed in two locations; it asks you to accept the child's other parent as an equally important force in her life and it asks you to establish a new business relationship with your co-parent in order to meet the needs of your child(ren). Realignment occurs after you have emotionally let go and disengaged from the former partner. Realignment means that you put aside negative assumptions and expectations about your co-parent's ability to parent. It means changing your language patterns to reflect acceptance for this new family structure. It means evaluating all actions in terms of your child's best interests over those your own self-interests. And it means using the STP-A technique to stop, think, then pause before taking any action which could be detrimental to your child.

Review if you're following these guidelines for a successful business relationship with your co-parent and identify where it needs improvement:

1. Dedication to a common goal.

2. Commitment to a win-win relationship.

3. Negotiation of differences when you disagree or when new circumstances arise.

4. Focus on a limited number of topics and objectives.

5. Observation of common courtesies.

6. Communication with facts rather than feelings.

Chapter 5: Managing My Own Anger

Chapter 5 asks you to see anger as a potential constructive force or a destructive force. When constructive, it gives you the power to take an action which may be difficult for you. It can be a motivator, pushing you to overcome obstacles and helping you reach your goals. It can give you the strength to set limits, assert yourself or take actions which will solve the problems that initially caused the anger.

Anger can also be destructive. Anger can be used to begin a cycle of revenge, taking actions which cause pain. Anger can motivate you to retaliate for real or perceived threats and result in escalating the problem it was designed to solve. In an effort to protect yourself from hurt or pain, you can use anger to hurt others, including yourself and your child. Anger can be turned inward, resulting in depression or feelings of paralysis, preventing you from taking actions required to solve the problem which cause the initial pain. Staying stuck in anger is a way of refusing to take responsibility for whatever problem is causing you the pain. When anger is used destructively, the child is hurt most of all.

The first step in using anger constructively is to **realize that what you do with anger is your choice.** Anger can provide you with an awareness that something is wrong; it becomes your first sign that you need to take action to solve a problem. It may indicate that your own limits are being assaulted and you need to be assertive in redefining where those limits are. Managing your anger means accepting responsibility for the results.

Then you need to identify the trigger that set you off. The next step is to identify beliefs or the thoughts set off by that trigger. These beliefs or thoughts are the ones that cause your feelings of anger to intensify. (Remember: it's not the traffic jam, it's what you **think** about the traffic jam that gets you upset.) When you can catch yourself before reacting to the anger, you can examine your beliefs and see if they can be changed or reframed into something more empowering.

Altering your beliefs will alter the intensity of the hurt or angry feelings which in turn will influence your actions. "He's so rotten, I'm going back to court to get more money and hurt him even more," will get you worked up. "I can't make him act a certain way, but I can decide how I will act," will calm you and help you make good decisions.

Chapter 6: Taking Control of Conflict

In this chapter we looked at how conflicts happen, how they start with little sparks and what happens next to keep them burning. First we looked at "fire prevention" techniques. These three W's make a difference in preventing conflict from starting.

Decide:

> • W = When to talk
> • W = What to talk about
> • W = Where to talk

When you set up the discussion mechanics carefully, you're more likely to avoid the conflict altogether.

The next guideline is to Avoid Playing with Matches. These are the things that set off sparks. They can consist of a tone of voice, a particular body language that is disrespectful or words that trigger the co-parent's anger. While you can't be responsible for another person's feelings and actions, sometimes you can choose to stay clear of the things that that you know will result in conflict.

The last guideline is to Avoid Throwing Fuel on the Fire. These are the responses to a lighted match set out by a co-parent. Without fuel the little flame will go out; with added fuel, the little flame can start a forest fire. Follow these guidelines: **Do not be defensive; do not counterattack or withdraw**. Instead, use STP-A to give yourself time to consider just what way you want to react to the sparks.

Decide how you want your voice to sound, which words you'll choose and what body language you'll use in making your response. This way you control the situation; the situation doesn't control you. Remove yourself if the co-parent is threatening or aggressive. Listen to and reflect what the co-parent says. Look for a feeling behind the words or action which shows your understanding of the other person's concerns. You can still disagree, and use good listening skills.

Also remember the 3 P's:

- Focus on the present not the past
- Focus on the problem not the person
- Focus on one problem not the universe

Use "I" statements to introduce the problem or to follow up with your own opinion of the problem. Lead with your concern for your child and explain how your child could be affected by the situation. Then suggest what you think is preferable instead. Remember, however, some situations are not within your area of control and you may just have to live with them. You may not like what happens in your co-parent's house, but unless it is directly detrimental to the child (use of drugs for example), don't move into an area where you shouldn't go. It's what is called a topic of non-interference. You can explain your concerns and your opinion but you can't force a solution that meets your needs. Nonetheless you may personally feel better by asserting your concerns and opinion. Then it is time to let it go.

"I" Statement Format

I feel . . . .

when . . . .

because . . . .

What I'd like is . . . .

Can you agree to that?

Chapter 7: Negotiating Agreements

To put what you learned in Chapter 7 into action, you first must **accept that if one parent "wins," not only does the other parent lose, but the child loses most.** When one parent "wins," that person is putting his own self-interest before the child's best interest. The only way for there to be a winner when there's a problem to solve is if everyone wins by finding the best solution for the child.

Negotiating agreement asks you to follow these steps:

Seven Steps to Negotiate Agreements

1. Name the problem
- call for an appointment
- use "I" statements

2. Give opinion; Reflect opinion
- take turns sharing your viewpoint followed by the other person reflecting your viewpoint

---

Seven Steps to Negotiate Agreements *(continuation)*

3. Brainstorm Solutions

- brainstorm without evaluating

4. Choose a Solution

- find the best solution for the child

5. Review

- who does what, by when

6. Put the Solution into Action

- try the best idea for a limited time period

7. Re-evaluate

- meet to discuss the successes

In this last chapter the focus will be on solving the real problems that are relevant to your personal situation. It's time to put your new skills to the test. The goal of this unique parenting guide is to change your way of communicating with the co-parent. Therefore, the skills need to be used frequently in order to become more effective. Don't be surprised if the first several times you try this on your own that it does not go smoothly. That's OK—just keep working on the skills. It should get easier with time and practice. If this is not the case in your situation, however, seek assistance from a trained parent coordinator or psychotherapist. A court-ordered parent coordinator will require both parents to cooperate and to learn the skills outlined in this book. **Remember any improvement will be worth it to your child.**

Weekly Co-Parent Meetings

Just as efficient businesses rely on regularly scheduled meetings, so do efficient households. Many families have discovered the benefit of weekly meetings to discuss such things as car pool needs, errands, discipline problems and shared family goals. This is especially true for the busy dual career family. The more limited your time, and the more stress in your family, the more important it is to have regularly scheduled family meetings. In a similar fashion, the binuclear or "two-home family" benefits from discussions regarding child-rearing matters. These meetings may be very brief, but should be done on a regular basis to help the two households run smoothly and minimize stress for the children. Unless you and your co-parent experience extremely conflicted interactions, plan on weekly telephone contact. Jointly select a day and time on a weekly basis to discuss the business of co-parenting your children. Be very specific regarding these plans. Topics of discussion might include:

- **Schedule Changes:**

  "Remember Ian does not have scouts this week."

- **Schedule Change Requests:**

  "Would it be OK with you if we changed the drop off time next Saturday to 7:30 pm instead of 6:00 pm?"

- **Notification/Reminders of Special Activities:**

  "Janice has a recital on Friday evening."

- **Management of Discipline Problems:**

  "Frankie got in trouble at school for throwing rocks at children. I'd like us to jointly come up with a consequence for his behavior and then follow through in both homes. What consequence do you think would be an appropriate?"

- **Sharing of Developmental Milestones and Accomplishments:**

  "Catherine can dress herself now. She is very proud of herself!" Or, "Thomas has started to learn how to ride a two wheeler bike. Can you help him practice this weekend?"

At first, the co-parenting discussion should be very brief and focus on simple matters or the sharing of positive experiences involving the children. Also consider the following tips:

Designate a weekly phone time with a window of approximately 30-minutes in length. For instance,

> Sunday evenings from 9:00 pm - 9:30 pm. Some calls may be as brief as a minute or take the full time.

Choose a time that is convenient for both parents and a time that limits the possibility of the children being present or overhearing the conversation.

Adhere to this schedule for a limited amount of time to determine if it works.

For example,

> Suggest that you try the scheduled conversation for the next four Sundays and then jointly re-evaluate.

> Mutually agree that scheduled phone calls will be ended if they become counter productive. However, if a conversation is cut short, a new date and time should be selected to continue the discussion ASAP.

It is very important to determine which parent will initiate the phone call and build in contingency plans in the event that one or both parents is not available or has forgotten the scheduled meeting. For instance

> The parent who physically has the children on the designated day initiates the phone call. This ensures that the children will not be present during the phone meeting.

> If the receiving parent is not available during the designated period of time when possible, the initiating parent should leave a message indicating that a call was made. The receiving parent should return the call the same evening whenever possible within a reasonable time frame. If the receiving parent is unable to make this return call, they are responsible for making the phone call the next day at the same time.

> If the initiating parent forgets or is unable to initiate the call, they become responsible for contacting the co-parent the next day.

> In the event that the initiating parent does not have a parenting issue to discuss, they

will still contact the co-parent to determine if there are any concerns that the other parent may want to discuss.

Although these regularly scheduled co-parenting meetings are intended to be short and sweet, there may be times when a more complicated or sensitive issue may need to be resolved. The following five steps will assist you and your co-parent to increase the likelihood of a successful interaction on serious or complex issues that have been difficult to discuss in the past.

Time to Solve Problems

1. Creating and Rating a List

If you recall, you were asked to notice which parenting concerns are problems between you and your co-parent. You were asked to keep a list on page 19 and then again on page 153. Some of these may be minor issues, such as how the child is transported to school, or major problems such as who will pay for the child's braces. Flip back to page 153 and select three to five of them. Take the time to list below each concern. Use a few words to describe the situation. Then, using a 1 to 5 rating scale, rate the most important concern a 5 and the least important or minor concern a 1. Write the numbers 1 to 5 in the column on the right. This will help you to know which problems you will need to address with your co-parent.

PROBLEMS TO RESOLVE

PROBLEM   **RATING (1-5)**

1. _____

_____

_____

2. _____

_____

_____

3. _____

_____

_____

4. _____

_____

_____

5. _____

_____

_____

2. Preparing the Negotiation Worksheet

Now that you have listed your concerns and have identified the most important issues, it is time to put the skills you have learned into action. Your long-term goal is to prepare yourself to negotiate agreements with your co-parent. When you make your first attempt at negotiating, it is easier to start with a simple issue or minor concern. Begin by selecting a problem you rated as a 1.

Before you begin, however, make several copies of the Negotiation Worksheet on page 173. To prepare for a co-parent discussion, complete Step #1 on your worksheet. You will notice that Step #1 has three important parts. Each of these parts needs to be completed prior to your meeting.

Step #1. Name the Problem

A. What is the Problem?

Decide which problem you will focus on first. Use a few words to describe the situation. Do this now on the negotiation worksheet.

B. Is the problem self or child-focused?

Review your problem and ask yourself:

1) How does the problem affect my child?

2) Is solving the problem in my own self-interest or in my child's best interest?

If you determine that the problem has more to do with your own self-interest rather than your child's best interest, select a different problem.

C. Create an "I" Statement:

Go over the problem you described and write down what you will say using the "I" statement format.

---

3. Structuring the Meeting

Now that you have prepared your worksheet, it is important to set the stage for a successful encounter with your co-parent. First, reflect on typical interactions that occur between you and your co-parent and the results of your attempts to negotiate. Below are some behaviors indicative of high conflict. Under these circumstances, it is important to structure the meeting very carefully. Determine if these behaviors are characteristic and frequently part of your interactions with your co-parent.

- arguments in front of the child
- arguments on the phone when the child is able to hear the conversations
- relentless demands
- verbal abuse (name-calling)
- physical attacks toward either parent
- physical attacks directed at the child
- threats to go back to court
- threats to leave town
- threats to harm the child
- threats to withhold money/visitation
- threats to withhold the child's love for the other parent

CAUTION

If your situation includes any of the following, we highly recommend that you seek the services of a neutral third party trained in conflict management and mediation such as a Parent Coordinator.

- History of violence or abuse
- Current alcohol or drug abuse
- Protective Order or Criminal charges

After assessing your co-parent relationship, consider the following recommendations:

Dangerous Duos: Relationship that has the potential for physical danger:

- Phone meetings scheduled during office hours
- Meetings with a third party to facilitate a safe and productive encounter

Adversarial Associates: Relationship with a pattern of intermittent conflict and/or verbal abuse:

- Phone meetings scheduled during office hours
- Brief meetings in a public place such as a restaurant during day time hours
- Meetings with a third party to facilitate a safe and productive encounter

Cautious Colleagues: Relationship characterized by patterns of mild to moderate conflict that are usually brought under control:

- Phone meetings scheduled during office hours
- Scheduled meetings in a public place during day time hours
- Extended meetings to discuss multiple issues

If your meeting goes well, do not move to additional concerns until you have asked yourself:

- Is the parent who brought up the concern satisfied that the issue has been addressed and that a plan has been worked out in detail?

- Is it a good time to address another issue? Your co-parent may not be up for another round of negotiation, or may not have the time to address a second issue. For these reasons, always ask before you lead into another parenting concern

- Has a break occurred before addressing a second concern? Change the subject for a brief period of time or get up and get a beverage so it does not feel like you are bombarding the co-parent with one issue after another

No matter how you structure the meeting, always keep these two points foremost in your mind:

① **Never discuss important matters with your co-parent by phone or in person when your child is present or awake.**

② **Always be prepared to disengage when the meeting is no longer productive. For instance,**

- if your co-parent continues to be loud after you have asked her to stop
- if your co-parent continues to talk over you after you have asked him to discontinue, or
- if your co-parent seems to be losing his temper and acting in an aggressive manner

In these situations, calmly end the meeting. To disengage say, *"I don't think this is productive. I would like to schedule another meeting. I will call you tomorrow."* Walking away without making a similar statement will only fuel the fire.

4. Arranging the Meeting

Once you have determined the structure for the meeting, arrange the meeting with your co-parent. You may start by suggesting a time and a place for the meeting (or phone call) that will be convenient for both of you. Your co-parent may be interested in knowing the purpose of the meeting. However, identifying the problem may open up the conversation prematurely and, as a result, you may not be prepared to effectively discuss the matter. Use your judgment about identifying the issue during your initial phone call. If you do, consider saying, *"I will briefly tell you my concern. I hope you don't mind if we wait to discuss it when we meet."* Stick to your guns. Avoid being pressured into a conversation at this time.

After the meeting, it is important to evaluate your behavior. Start by asking yourself: What went well and what didn't? Consider your tone of voice. Was it sarcastic or threatening or even and calm? Did I focus on the problem rather than my co-parent? Did I use body language which invited problem-solving or did it invite aggression or defensive maneuvers? Did I use the seven steps to solve the problem, suggesting alternative solutions and respecting my co-parent's opinions? Did I judge the brainstorming ideas of my co-parent? Did I use good business skills or did I let my emotions do the talking?

An honest evaluation of your behavior will better prepare you for co-parent discussions in the future.

If your encounter with your co-parent did not go as well as you hoped, do not despair. Remember, it should get easier with time and practice. Next time, consider doing one or more of the following:

- Say less, listen more.
- Stay calmer; breathe deeply.
- Increase your empathetic responses: *"I can see why you would really be upset by that."*
- Remove yourself sooner.
- Act optimistic, "We'll just try this later."
- Change the time and/or location of the meeting.
- Take control of conflict by reviewing and using the skills outlined in chapter six.
- Invite your co-parent, if they are not part of a mandated program, to read chapters six and seven before your next attempt to negotiate problems.
- Add a neutral third party.

Ways I Can Improve the Outcome of Our Future Interactions

List a few ways that you can improve the outcome of future interactions with your co-parent.

_____

_____

_____

Dedication to the Future

The two most important factors for a healthy co-parent relationship are your commitment to being child-focused and your ability to let go of your negative emotions. Doing all that you can to disengage from your former spouse will benefit you and your child. As you recall, we presented a ritual to help you release yourself from the former relationship with your former spouse. We called it a Letting-Go Ritual. You may remember reading about it in Chapter 3. In a similar manner, the following ritual is intended to help you let go of the past.

Marriage Balloon

This ritual can be done with one or both parents. Write your wedding date on a small piece of paper and allow the children to witness you put it into a helium balloon and release it. For your child's sake, it helps to say something good about the marriage before releasing the "marriage." When the balloon is out of sight, tell the children that the marriage is over. End on a positive note by going for ice cream or somewhere special to mark a new beginning. If you do this ritual without your co-parent, very young children may think that you are getting rid of their other parent when you release the balloon. Therefore, it is better to do this ritual with both parents present. If that is not possible, make sure that you make it clear to your child that they still have two parents. Keep the ritual positive even if tears are shed.

The following rituals also focus on releasing the marital relationship while focusing on a positive future.

Three Candles:

Both parents must be present during this ritual and it is intended to be witnessed by the children. Light a candle to represent your marriage. Each parent lights an individual candle from the marriage candle to represent their life as a separate individual. Then, both parents place their individual candles in separate candle holders and together blow out the marriage candle. Do not let your child participate in blowing out the marriage candle. This must be done by the parents. Words may be added at any point.

The Ring Ceremony:

This ritual is designed for both parents and the children. The children witness both parents returning their wedding rings in exchange for a token of commitment to co-parenting. For example, you can prepare a written agreement or a certificate with the children's pictures on it.

Both the candle and the ring ceremony can be combined with the following activity that uses a certificate found on page 181. The **"Co-Parenting Is Forever"** certificate can be used to signify your realignment to a co-parent relationship and your commitment to your children. No matter how long you have been divorced, this ritual can be very useful to you and your family. It asks you to make decisions based on your child's needs and to work together as a team to meet those needs. It asks you to commit yourselves as individuals as well as partners in parenting to meeting these goals. Ideally, both parents should be willing participants. However, if your co-parent chooses not to participate, do it on your own.

This ritual can be done in many different ways. Keep the activity child-focused while reassuring your children that you will be their parents forever. Consider doing the following:

- Present the "Co-Parenting Is Forever" certificate to your children together.
- Read it to them.
- Ask them to sign as a witness (just like a marriage certificate).

- Copy it if you have more than one child. Your child may want you to laminate it.

- Attach the Divorce Rules on page 17 on the back of their certificate before laminating it.

- Tell your child that he may keep the certificate to remind him that, even though his parents are divorced, he will always have both of you.

- Reassure her that you both have learned new behaviors and that you are committed to making things better.

- For a more intimate and spiritual ceremony refer to *Illuminata*, by Marianne Williamson.

Vision of the Future

Fostering Shared Activities

Take a few minutes now and look toward the future. Get a picture in your mind of the following scene. See your child performing on stage and you and your co-parent sitting in the audience. Watch your child as he moves his head from side to side to find both of you and make eye contact. See exactly how hard she has to work to seek you out. Now, picture yourself sitting closer to your co-parent in the audience and focusing on your child. See how your child now has an easier time focusing on his own performance because it takes less effort to locate you and keep you in his line of sight. Now go one step further and visualize yourself sitting in the same row with your child's other parent, maybe just a few seats apart.

Embracing Your Child's Extended Family

As you visualize a successful co-parenting relationship, consider the extended relationships that make up your child's family. Allow your child to maintain contact with both sets of grandparents and significant relatives. After all, they are still part of your child's family. Each grandparent offers something special to your child. There are many ways grandparents can contribute to your child's well-being. Sense of family and time-honored traditions are a few ways. Now go back to your child's performance and imagine your co-parent's extended family sharing in this special day. Visualize yourself inviting your former in-laws to your child's recital! How many people love your child? Remember, your child can be enriched through their contact with their extended family.

Preparing For Situational Changes

Suppose you or the co-parent receive a career promotion. How might this pose a threat? A promotion of one or both parents may negatively impact the stability of the co-parent relationship. A career opportunity may necessitate a move by one parent. The children may have to establish a long-distance relationship with one parent. As a result, new time-sharing arrangements may have to be agreed upon.

Take another look toward the future. Visualize yourself remarrying. Although your new marriage may be looked upon with great anticipation, don't be surprised if you once again grieve the loss of your former marriage. Remarriage may also require you to establish new ways of communicating with your co-parent. Now imagine your co-parent announcing that she is getting married and the potential emotional impact of hearing this news.

A remarriage has a significant impact on a child. He will need to determine where he fits in the new family structure. In one family she may be the oldest child, but in her second family she may be a middle child. Everyone will need time to adjust, whether you are the parent getting married or not. Loyalty binds may resurface. Children may feel caught between their love for their biological parent and their fondness for a step-parent. As a result they may play down their feelings for the step-parent in order to protect their natural parent. Children are acutely aware of "fairness." If one parent remarries and the other doesn't, it increases the likelihood that the child will care for the single parent, especially if they view this parent as a victim. Remember, this is not in your child's best interest.

Navigating Developmental Changes

Your child's changing developmental needs and interests will also place different demands on your relationship. Co-parents may have to modify their child's schedule to take into consideration these changes. The best guideline to follow is one that allows your child to benefit from a close and satisfying relationship with both parents. Such an arrangement often means that you will have to make the effort to remain close to the co-parent geographically. Upholding a successful co-parent relationship requires many tests of flexibility and sensitivity.

As your child grows and matures, you and the co-parent will be faced with different issues at each stage of development. Each of these transitions demand continued communication and effective negotiation skills. When will your child be allowed to attend over-night camps, get her ears pierced, or begin dating? At what age will your teenager be allowed to attend unsupervised rock concerts, date or wear make-up? You may not realize the multiple issues that can arise during the teen years. For example, how will you negotiate conflicting parental values around issues such as body piercing and tattoos? What arrangements will be made for the child's college education? What types of standards will be established once your child ventures out on his own? These are just a few of the questions you and your co-parent will face as your child matures and grows. Again, take the next step and visualize a future of promise and opportunities. See yourself using the knowledge and skills you have learned to continually meet the challenges of maintaining a strong co-parent relationship throughout the life of your child.

Give the Gift of a Strong Co-parent Relationship

Everyone likes giving (and getting) gifts. When you give your child the gift of a strong co-parent relationship you are truly giving her one of the best gifts a parent can ever give. You are removing stress and self-doubt. You are helping strengthen your child's identity. You are allowing your child to love both parents and himself, fully. You are building your child's belief in himself and his world. Please dedicate yourself to this important goal. No one else can give this gift. No one but you can make this decision. Your child's future depends on it.

Dear Mom and Dad,

I can't tell you how proud I am to have you as a parent! Taking the time to read this book has meant so much to me. You have really made some changes and I know that you will continue to improve things for me. You must really love me. Thanks!

Forever grateful,

Your loving child
XXXXXXOOOOOO

Chapter Eight Review

1   What parts of the negotiation worksheet should be completed before you sit down with your co-parent to discuss a parenting concern?

2.   Why is it valuable to structure parenting meetings?

3.   Have you anticipated future problem areas so you and your co-parent will be ready to handle them together as they arise?

4.   Are you able to distinguish a "personal" issue from a "parenting" issue?

5.   How have you emotionally prepared yourself for potential setbacks that may occur as your child's needs and interests change? How have you emotionally prepared yourself for significant changes that occur in your co-parent's life as well?

6.   Do you and your co-parent conduct weekly business meetings by phone or in person? If so, how would you rate your joint ability to resolve parenting matters in this format?

7.   As you look into the future, will you and your co-parent be able to share in life-long activities with your child as they grow into adulthood?

NEGOTIATION WORKSHEET

STEP #1. NAME THE PROBLEM

A. Problem

_____

_____

_____

B. How it impacts our child

_____

_____

_____

Child-Focused _____ Self-Focused _____

C. Create an "I" Statement

I feel/felt _____

when _____

because _____

and what I'd like is _____

STEP #2. REFLECT (then share opinion-reflect)

STEP #3. BRAINSTORM SOLUTIONS (don't evaluate them)

a. _____

b. _____

c. _____

d. _____

e. _____

STEP #4. CHOOSE A SOLUTION (find the best solution for your child)

_____

_____

_____

STEP #5. REVIEW (who does what by when?)

_____

_____

STEP #6. ACTION (time limit)

_____

_____

STEP #7. RE-EVALUATE

Date _____

TWO HOME COMMUNICATION MEMOS

The following "memos" can be used to notify your co-parent of significant events in your child's life, to request a change in time-sharing arrangements and to clarify agreements. Parents experiencing highly conflicted relationships can use these memos to establish information sharing while minimizing face to face contact. Mail or fax these memos to your co-parent.

"Confirmation Memo"

Dear Co-Parent;

In an attempt to work together for our children, this is a courtesy reminder.

Our child _____ *has an activity of*
             Child's name

_____ *on*_____ *at*
        Activity

_____.

☐ *Additional information attached*   ☐ *Hope to see you there*

Signed _____

Dated _____

"Location Notification"

Dear Co-Parent;

This memo is an attempt to be respectful and to keep you informed of my location in case of an emergency. I will be out of town on the following dates _____ and may be reached at the following phone number _____.

(OR)

Dear Co-Parent;

This memo is to keep you informed of the children's location. We will be away from home on the following dates _____. The children may be reached at the following phone number _____.

Signed _____

Dated _____

"Request for Change"

Dear Co-Parent;

I am respectfully requesting the following change to our child's time share arrangement. I would like to request the following change:

_____   _____
Original Dates   *Original Times*

_____   _____
Requested Dates   *Requested Times*

I am requesting this change for the following reason(s)

_____

_____

_____

Please consider this request and get back to me by _____ so we can make the necessary changes. Otherwise, I will assume that this request has been denied and will stay with the original schedule. Thanks for your cooperation.

☐ *If necessary, I am willing to arrange an equal exchange*   ☐ *Call to discuss further*

Signed _____

Dated _____

"Shared Decision Memo"

Dear Co-Parent;

I am considering _____

for our child _____. *This would occur on the*

following dates _____. *The cost is* $ _____

☐ *I am requesting your feedback regarding this proposal*

☐ *I am requesting your financial assistance*

☐ *I am assuming I will pay for this under our normal agreement*

If I do not hear back from you by _____ *I will assume you* **do
not object to this idea** *and I will proceed. However, it would be best to discuss this
matter directly. I hope that you will support this plan. Let me know, ASAP.*

Signed _____

Dated _____

"Medical Notification"

Dear Co-Parent;

It is important that you know _____ *has been ill with*
Child's name

_____ .
Child's symptoms

He/she is currently taking the following medication(s) _____

_____ .

On the following schedule _____ .

_____ .

    ☐ *He/she had a doctor's appointment on* _____

    ☐ *He/she will see the doctor on* _____

    ☐ *The medication was prescribed by the doctor.*

        ☐ *Only as needed* _____

        ☐ *Every* _____

    ☐ *Since it is an antibiotic, he/she must finish the entire bottle*

    ☐ *The medication is over the counter and needs to be administered*

        ☐ *Only as needed* _____

        ☐ *Every* _____

Other instructions include:

_____

_____

As always, thanks for working with me.

Signed _____

Dated _____

"Offer for Additional Time"
(first right of refusal)

Dear Co-Parent;

Although our child/ren are scheduled to be with me on _____

_____

I will be unavailable to keep them due to _____

_____

Since the child/ren should have an opportunity to be with you rather than someone else, I am informing you of the situation first. Unless I hear from you by

_____, *I will make other arrangements for the children at my expense. As always, I will let you know where they will be during this time.*

Signature _____

Date _____

"Management Memo"

Dear Co-Parent;

It is important that you be aware of the following management problems that our child,

_____, is having.

I have been notified by the school that our child is experiencing the following difficulties at school:

_____

_____

_____

☐ *School performance has dropped*
☐ *Not turning in homework or completing school work*
☐ *Peer related problems*
☐ *School behavioral problems*
☐ *Seems to need tutoring in* _____

Home Management problems include:

_____

_____

_____

In an attempt to work as a team to help our child, I would suggest we

    ☐ *Meet to discuss this further*
    ☐ *We both do the following* _____

_____

I will plan to use the following consequences/motivators to address the school problems,

_____

_____

I will plan to use the following consequences/motivators to address the home problems,

_____

_____

Since I respect your parenting input, let me know your thoughts and your willingness to join me in this effort. If both of us use similar management techniques, we will be better able to help our child achieve personal goals. Please call to discuss this further. Thanks for your consideration.

Signed _____ *Dated* _____

Co-Parenting Is Forever

Recognizing that co-parenting is forever,
we agree to cooperate on behalf of our child(ren).

We will allow our child(ren) to love both parents.

_____
Mother

_____
Witness

_____
Father

_____
Date

AUTHOR INFORMATION

Susan Boyan and Ann Marie Termini are co-founders of Cooperative Parenting Institute. Their mission is to promote the healing and enhancement of family relationships and to focus their work on educating others regarding the effects of divorce and time-sharing arrangements on the development of children. C.P.I. provides the most promising solutions for separating families through confidential psychotherapy, seminars, publications and the media. The professionals at C.P.I. have been actively involved in developing a continuum of services for families in transition including work as court ordered Parent Coordinators. They have also written a book to assist divorcing parents with preschool children. It is a combination text and parent/child workbook entitled *"Parents R Forever: Everything You Need to Know to Help Your Young Child Adjust to Divorce."* Widely known for their expertise in the area of divorce and the family, the authors consult extensively with family law professionals, make radio and television appearances, and provide training and consultation to educators, family law and mental health professionals.

Susan Boyan, M.Ed., is a Licensed Marriage and Family Therapist. She has worked with children and families since 1971 and has been in private practice since 1984. Mrs. Boyan is a clinical member in the American Association for Marriage and Family Therapy. She is also a member and research chair for the Georgia Play Therapy Association. She is also a member of Association of Family and Conciliation Courts, Association of Fathers and Children, Step Family Association, Association of Christian Counselors, Southeast Psychomotor Society and the National Association for Children of Alcoholics. She consults extensively and presents numerous professional presentations to national, state and local audiences. Mrs. Boyan does expert witness testimony and has written articles on Parental Alienation. She was a former special education teacher and rehabilitation counselor. Mrs. Boyan divorced in 1979. In 1981 she married and has two beautiful daughters. She resides in Atlanta, Georgia, with her family.

Ann Marie Termini, Ed.S., M.S., is a Licensed Professional Counselor. She has worked with children and families since 1979. Respected in her field, she has conducted numerous seminars on the national, state and local levels. She has experience developing programs that meet the specific needs of professionals working with children and their families. Mrs. Termini also published material in professional journals focusing on the therapeutic needs of children. She was a former officer for the San Antonio Association for Marriage and Family Therapy and coordinator for special education services. She has been awarded Clinical Membership in the American Association for Marriage and Family Therapy. Among her many professional activities, Mrs. Termini is a consultant for a family court in Pennsylvania and maintains a private practice. She resides in Clarks Summit, Pennsylvania, with her husband and two lovely daughters.

Authors may be reached at www.cooperativeparenting.com

RESOURCES

SUGGESTED READING FOR PARENTS

Anger, Conflict Management, and Negotiation

Glass, Lillian. *Ten Ways of Dealing with People Who Make Your Life Miserable.* New York: St. Martin's Griffin, 1995.

Fisher, Roger, and William Ury. *Getting to Yes: Negotiating Agreement Without Giving In.* New York: Viking Penguin, 1981.

Elgin, Suzette Hoden. *The Gentle Art of Verbal Self-Defense.* John Wiley & Sons.

Elgin, Suzette Hoden. *You Can't Say That to Me: Stopping the Pain of Verbal Abuse.* John Wiley & Sons, 1995.

Kersey, Katharine. *Helping Your Child Handle Stress.*

Kline, Kris; and Pew, Stephen. *For the Sake of the Children: How to Share Your Children with Your Ex-Spouse in Spite of Your Anger.* California: Prima Publishing, 1992.

Lerner, Harriet Goldhor. *The Dance of Anger: A Woman's Guide to Changing Patterns of Intimate Relationships.* New York: Harper & Row Perennial, 1986.

McKnew, Donald; Cytryn, Leo; and Yahraes, Herbert. *Why Isn't Johnny Crying?*

Tavris, Carol. *Anger: The Misunderstood Emotion.*

Weeks, Dudley. *The Eight Essential Steps to Conflict Resolution: Preserving Relationships at Work, at Home, and in the Community.* California: Tarcher, 1992.

Youngs, Bettie B. *Stress in Children.*

Change and Forgiveness

Beattie, Melody. *The Language of Letting Go.* New York: Harper Collins, 1990.

Colgrove, Melda and Bloomfield, Harold. *How To Survive the Loss of a Love.* Bantam Books, 1977.

Fisher, Bruce. *Rebuilding: When Your Relationship Ends.* California: Impact Publishers, 1982.

Jampolsky, Gerald. *Love is Letting Go of Fear.* Clestrail Arts, 1979.

Lerner, Harriet Goldhor. *The Dance of Intimacy: A Woman's Guide to Courageous Acts of Change in Key Relationships.* New York: Harper & Row, 1989.

Mason, Marilyn J. *Making Our Lives Our Own: A Women's Guide to the Six Challenges of Personal Change.* California: Harper San Francisco, 1991.

Napolitane, C. *Living and Loving after Divorce.* New York: Signet, 1977.

Passick, Robert, Ph.D. *Awakening from the Deep Sleep: A Powerful Guide for Courageous Men.* California: Harper San Francisco, 1992.

Rogers, John and McWilliams. *You Can't Afford the Luxury of a Negative Thought.* Prelude Press, Inc., 1989.

Seligman, Martin. *Learned Optimism: How To Change Your Mind and Your Life*. Pocket Books, 1990.

Simon, Sidney. *Getting Unstuck: Breaking Through Your Barriers to Change*. New York: Warner Books, 1988.

Simon, Sidney. F*orgiveness: How to Make Peace with Your Past and Get On with Your Life*. New York: Warner Books, 1990.

Smedes, Lewis, B. *Forgive & Forget*. New York: Pocket Books, 1984.

Stearns, Ann Kaiser. *Living Through Personal Crisis*. Chicago: Thomas Moore Press, 1984.

Steinem, Gloria. *Revolution From Within*. Boston: Little, Brown, 1992.

Vaughn, Diane. *Uncoupling: Turning Points in Intimate Relationships*. New York: Vintage Books, 1990.

Viorst, Judith. *Necessary Losses: The Loves, Illusions, Dependencies and Impossible Expectations That All of Us Have to Give Up in Order to Grow*. New York: Ballantine, 1986.

Weiss, Robert S. *Marital Separation: Coping with the End of a Marriage and the Transition to Being Single Again*. New York: Basic Books, 1975.

Divorce:

Blau, Melinda. *Families Apart: Ten Keys to Successful Co-Parenting*. New York: Putman, 1993.

Blau, Melinda. Loving and Listening: *A Book of Daily Inspiration for Rebuilding the Family After Divorce*.

Boyan, Susan and Termini, Ann Marie. *Parents R Forever*. Family Solutions LLC (1997).

Cohen, Miriam Galper. *The Joint Custody Handbook*. Philadelphia: Running Press, 1991.

Cohen, Miriam Galper. *Long-Distance Parenting: A Guide for Divorced Parenting*. New York: New American Library, 1989.

Diamond, S.A. *Helping Children of Divorce: A Handbook for Parents and Teachers*. New York: Shocken Books, 1985.

Gardner, Richard A. *The Parents' Book About Divorce*. New York: Bantam, 1977.

Hickey, Elizabeth and Dalton, Elizabeth. *Healing Hearts: Helping Children And Adults Recover from Divorce; Goldleaf Press*. 1994.

Jewett, C. *Helping Children Cope with Separation and Loss*. Cambridge, MA: Harvard University Press, 1982.

Johnson, Laurene and Rosenfeld, Georglynn. *What You Need to Know to Help Your Kid Survive a Divorce: Divorced Kids*. Fawcett Press, 1990.

Lansky, Vicki. *Vicki Lansky's Divorce Book for Parents*. New York: New American Library, 1989.

Levy, David L., ed. *The Best Parent Is Both Parents: A Guide to Shared Parenting in the 21st Century*. Norfolk, Va.: Hampton Roads Publishing Company, 1993.

Marston, Stephanie. *The Divorced Parent: Success Strategies for Raising Your Children After Separation*. New York: Morrow, 1994.

Newman, G. *101 Ways to Be a Long-Distance Superdad.* Mountain View, CA: Blossom Valley Press, 1984.

Oddenion, Michael. Putting Kids First: *Walking Away from a Marriage Without Walking Over the Kids.* Family Connections, 1995.

Ricci, Isolina. *Mom's House, Dad's House: Making Shared Custody Work.* New York: Macmillan, 1982, 1997.

Teyber, Edward. *Helping Your Children with Divorce.* New York: Pocket Books, 1985.

Teyber, Edward. *Helping Children Cope with Divorce.* New York: Lexington Books, 1992.

Walker, Glynnis. *Solomon's Children: Exploding the Myths of Divorce.* New York: Arbor House, 1986.

Ware, Ciji. *Sharing Parenthood after Divorce: An Enlightened Custody Guide for Mothers, Fathers, and Kids.* New York: Viking, 1982.

SUGGESTED READING FOR CHILDREN

Preschool:
Adams, Florence. *Mushy Eggs.* New York: Putnam, 1973.

Brown, Laurence and Laurence, Marc. *Dinosaurs Divorce.* New York: Little, Brown, 1968.

Cain, Barbara. *Double-Dip Feelings: Stories to Help Children Understand Emotions.*

Christiansen, C.B. *My Mother's House, My Father's House.* New York: Atheneum/ Macmillan, 1995.

Drescher, Joan. *Your Family, My Family.* New York: Walker, 1980.

Goff, Beth. *Where Is Daddy? The Story of a Divorce.* Boston: Beacon Press, 1969.

Hazen, Barbara S. *Two Homes to Live In: A Child's-Eye View of Divorce.* New York: Human Sciences Press, 1978.

Helmering, Doris. *I Have Two Families.* Nashville: Abingdon, 1981.

Schindel, John. *Dear Daddy.* Albert Whitman, 1995.

Simon, Norma. *I Wish I Had My Father.* Niles, Illinois: Whitman, 1983.

Sinberg, Janet. *Divorce is a Grown-up Problem.* New York: Avon, 1978.

Elementary School:
Berger, Terry. *How Does It Feel When Your Parents Get Divorced?* New York: Julian Messner, 1977.

Blue, Rose. *A Month of Sundays.* New York: Franklin Watts, 1972.

Blume, Judy. *It's Not the End of the World.* New York: Bradbury, 1972.

Boegehold, Betty. *Daddy Doesn't Live Here Anymore.* Racine, Wis.: Golden Books/ Western Publishing Company, 1985.

Brogan, J., and W. Maiden. *The Kid's Guide to Divorce*. New York: Fawcett, 1986.

Cleary, Beverly. *Dear Mr. Henshaw*. New York: Morrow.

Fassler, David, Michael Lash, and Sally Ives. *Changing Families*. Burlington, Vermont: Waterfront Books, 1988.

Field, Mary Blitzer and Shore, Hennie. *My Life Turned Upside Down, But I Turned It Right Side Up*. Center for Applied Psychology, Inc. 1994.

Gardner, Richard A. *The Boys and Girls Book About Divorce*. New York: Bantam, 1970.

Gerstein, Mordecai. *The Story of May*. New York: HarperCollins, 1993.

Girard, Linda. *At Daddy's On Saturdays*. Illinois: Albert Whitman, 1988.

Heegardd, M. When Mom and Dad Separate. Deaconess Press, 1992.

Ives, Fassler and Lash. *The Divorce Workbook: A Guide for Kids and Families*. Vermont: Waterfront Books, 1985.

Kagy-Taylor, Kathy, and Donna Marmer. *All About Change*. Cincinnati: Beech Acres, 1990.

Lasher, M. *My Kind of Family: A Book for Kids in Single-Parent Families*. Vermont: Waterfront Books, 1991.

Lebowitz, Marcia. *I Think Divorce Stinks*. Woodbridge, Connecticut: CDC Press, 1989.

LeShan, Eda. *What's Going to Happen to Me? When Parents Separate or Divorce*. New York: Macmillan, 1986.

Mayle, Peter. *Divorce Can Happen to the Nicest People*. New York: Macmillan, 1979.

Mayle, Peter. *Why Are We Getting A Divorce?* New York: Harmony Books, 1990.

Newfield, Marcia. *A Book for Jordan*. New York: Atheneum, 1975.

Park, Barbara. *Don't Make Me Smile*. New York: Knopf, 1981.

Richards, A., and Willis, I. *How to Get It Together When Your Parents Are Coming Apart*. New York: Mackay, 1976.

Sanford, D. *Please Come Home*. Colorado: Multnomah Press, 1988.

Sinberg, Janet. *Divorce Is a Grown-up Problem*. New York: Avon, 1978.

Stinson, Katherine. *Mom and Dad Don't Live Together Anymore*. New York: Annick Press, 1985.

Vigna, J. *Saying Goodbye to Daddy*. Illinois: Albert Whitman, 1991.

Preteen and Teenager:
Blume, Judy. *It's Not the End of the World*. New York: Dell, 1986.

Byars, B. *The Animal, the Vegetable, and John D. Jones*. New York: Delacorte, 1982.

Cleary, Beverly. *Dear Mr. Henshaw*. New York: William Morrow, 1983.

Danzier, Paula. *The Divorce Express*. New York: Delacorte, 1982.

Gardner, Richard A. *The Boys and Girls Book About Divorce*. New York: Bantam, 1970.

Goldman, Katie. *In the Wings*. New York: Dial, 1982.

Holland, Isabelle. *The Man Without a Face*. Philadelphia: Lippincott, 1972.

Klein, Norma. *Breaking Up*. New York: Avon, 1980.

Kline, Norma. *Taking Sides*. New York: Pantheon, 1974.

Krementz, Jill. *How It Feels When Parents Divorce*. New York: Alfred A. Knopf, 1988.

Oppenheimer, Joan L. *Gardine vs. Hanover*. New York: Crowell, 1982.

Stolz, Mary. *Look Before You Leap*. New York: Harper & Row, 1975.

BIBLIOGRAPHY

Arbuthnot, J. and Gordan, D.A. (1993). *What About the Children: A Guide for Divorced and Divorcing Parents.* Ohio: Center for Divorce Education.

Ahrons, C. (1994). *The Good Divorce: Keeping Your Family Together When Your Marriage Comes Apart. TGD*, 2nd Edition, Harper Collins.

Berger, S. (1983). *Divorce Without Victims.* Bosaton: Houghton Mifflin Company.

Blau, M. (1993). *Families Apart: Ten Keys to Successful Co-Parenting.* New York: Putman.

Buehler, C., Betz, P. Ryan, C., Legg, B. and Trotter, B. (1992). *Description and Evaluation of the Orientation for Divorcing Parents: Implications for PostDivorce Prevention Programs.* Family Relations, 41, 154-162.

Camera, K. and Resnick, G. (1988). *Interparental Conflict and Cooperation: Factors Mediating Children's Post Divorce Adjustment.* In E.M. Hetherington & J.D. Arasteh (Eds.) Impact of Divorce, Single Parenting and Stepparenting on Children. (pp. 169-195). New Jersey: Erlbaum.

Clapp, G. (1992). *Divorce & New Beginnings.* New York: John Wiley & Sons, Inc.

Covey, S.R. (1989). *The Seven Habits of Highly Effective People.* New York: Simon & Schuster.

Elgin, S. Haden. (1995). *You Can't Say That to Me!* New York: John Wiley & Sons, Inc.

Evans, P. (1992). *The Verbally Abusive Relationship.* Bob Adams, Inc.

Gardner, R. (1992). *The Parental Alienation Syndrome.* New Jersey: Creative Therapeutics.

Garrity, C. and Baris, M. (1994). *Caught in the Middle.* New York: Lexington Books.

Hetherington, E.M., Cox, M., and Cox, R. (1985). *Long-term Effects of Divorce and Remarriage on the Adjustment of Children.* Journal of the American Academy of Child Psychiatry, 24, 518-30.

Jarratt, C. (1982). *Helping Children Cope with Separation and Loss.* The Harvard Common Press.

Johnson, D. and Johnson, P. (1982). *Joining Together.* New Jersey: Englewood Press.

Johnston, J. and Campbell, L. (1988). *Impasses of Divorce.* New York: Free Press.

Kalter, N. (1990). *Growing Up With Divorce.* New York: The Free Press.

Marston, S. (1994). *The Divorced Parent: Success Strategies for Raising Your Children After Separation.* New York: William Marrow and Company.

Maccoby, E. and Mnookin, R. (1992). *Dividing the Child.* Cambridge: Harvard University Press.

McKay, M. and Rogers, P. (1989). *When Anger Hurts: Quieting the Storm Within.* New Harper Publishing Company.

Pittman, F. (1987). *Turning Points: Treating Families in Transition and Crisis.* W.W. Norton & Company.

Ricci, I. (1982). *Mom's House, Dad's House: Making Shared Custody Work.* New York: Simon & Schuster.

Walen, S., DiGiuseppe, R. and Wessler, R. (1980). *A Practitioner's Guide to Rational-Emotive Therapy.* New York: Oxford University Press.

Wallerstein, J. and Blakeslee, S. (1989). *Second Chances: Men, Women, and Children a Decade after Divorce.* New York: Ticknor and Fields.

COOPERATIVE PARENTING AGREEMENTS

Record the agreements made between you and your co-parent regarding your children.

Date   **Agreement**

Notes:

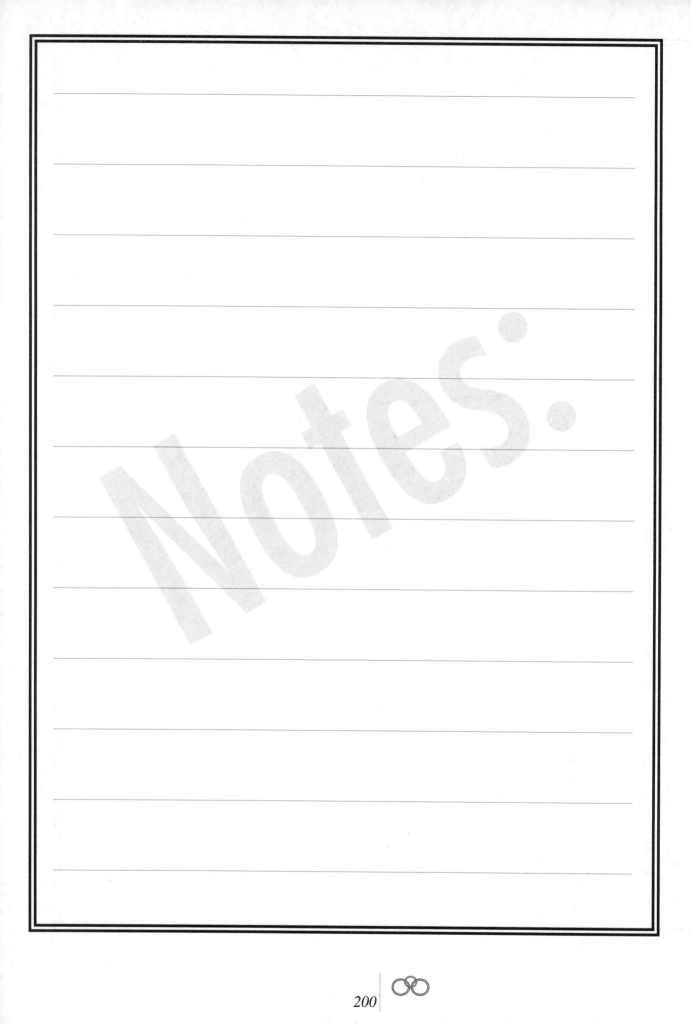

TRASH IT HERE

Throw all your old business in this trash can. Write your personal issues in the area below. This includes any hard feelings towards the co-parent that do not directly affect your child. These issues should not be discussed with your co-parent. Take the list to your personal counselor.

Active Parenting Publishers has additional resources to help parents with:

- Parenting Skills
- Self-Esteem Development
&
- Loss Education

For more information, contact:

Atlanta, Georgia
cservice@activeparenting.com • www.ActiveParenting.com
(800) 825-0060